GWR
COUNTRY STATIONS

GWR
COUNTRY STATIONS

CHRIS LEIGH

LONDON
IAN ALLAN LTD

First published 1981
Third impression 1985

ISBN 0 7110 1108 7

Published by Ian Allan Ltd, Shepperton, Surrey;
and printed by Ian Allan Printing Ltd at their works
at Coombelands in Runnymede, England

For James

Contents

Preface   6

Introduction   8

The Country Station   10

The Brunel Types   14

Early Standard Types   30

20th Century Standard Styles   43

Some Country Junctions   54

Subsidiary Buildings   60

Signalboxes   69

Goods Sheds   74

Inherited Station Buildings   80

Midland & South Western Junction
    Railway   97

Bristol & Exeter Railway   102

Berks & Hants Extension Railway   108

Oxford, Worcester & Wolverhampton
    Railway   114

A Special Favourite   125

Index   128

Title page: An evocative view of Bloxham which depicts so many of the features of a typical GWR country station, even down to the vegetable garden and 'standard' evergreen trees. *A. L. Ross*

Left: A typical rural halt seen in the days just prior to Beeching. A Pressed Steel single unit and trailer, forming a West Drayton-Staines West train, approaches Poyle Halt for Stanwell Moor. *Ian Allan Library*

Preface

In recent years there have been a few books published dealing with the subject of stations and railway architecture. In general they have either been books dealing in great detail with a specific branch line or minor railway, or sound architectural appreciations of the most imposing examples of railway architecture. They have made a welcome start in filling one of the gaps in railway literature which had hitherto concentrated rather more on locomotives and railway operation. Although the principal stations and many of the minor branch lines were thus well documented, there has been little coverage of the intermediate stations — the picturesque wayside stations which were just a blur from the carriage windows of a passing express. Many of these basked colourfully in their final summers during the early 1960s and possessed a character and charm which has failed to come across in much of the railway literature. Therein is the germ of this book.

While others very rightly recorded the demise of the steam locomotive and its associated paraphernalia, I was pointing my camera at the items of railway architecture which were vanishing equally quickly. Sadly, most of my efforts were in colour print form and this fact and the use of an inferior camera rendered many of them useless for publication. At least three attempts were made to start preparation of a book on Great Western stations, but only after the appearance of the three 'Western Country Stations' articles in *Railway World* (October and November 1978 and January 1979) did the book really start to take shape. Part of the text from those articles has been used here, amended as necessary, and much-expanded.

As a keen railway modeller the lack of building kits for genuine GWR structures has always surprised me, and even with the enormous amount of model equipment now available, there are still only a handful of such kits. With the modeller in mind I have included a number of drawings illustrating some of the distinctive GWR styles. Most of these have been selected because they are interesting and attractive structures, and also because many of the standard elements, such as doors and windows, can be used by the modeller in developing his own drawings of similar structures or in producing freelance designs with the correct appearance. Drawings of buildings are not produced by the precise science which can be applied to drawings of locomotives or rolling stock. In most cases original drawings no longer exist, structures have

been modified, or original design dimensions were altered 'on site' by the builder. Settlement of foundations can cause distortion of several inches, and a modification which has been well done can be indistinguishable from the original work. In addition, full dimensional surveys of most structures, particularly in relation to height measurements, are often impracticable. Climbing upon the roof of a structure to measure the chimney stacks is not to be recommended! Thus, the drawings have been reproduced from a combination of site measurements, known standard dimensions, and calculation from photographs. Where details are in doubt, these are mentioned in the accompanying text. Where possible drawings are reproduced to 4mm:1ft scale as this is the most popular for modelling. Larger structures are reduced to 2mm:1ft scale.

The first sections of the book deal with the development of 'standard' GWR architecture through typical wayside stations from the Brunel era to the 1930s. Signalboxes, goods sheds, and miscellaneous buildings are covered briefly and the final sections deal with some of the attractive non-standard structures peculiar to particular sections of line, or inherited by the GWR from constituent companies. In my view, there is no real substitute for personal knowledge of a station and for this reason the most detailed coverage is given to those stations which I knew particularly well. For the same reason, and because it was not practical to cover the whole of the Western Region in the time available during the mid-1960s, Wales is largely omitted.

During that period I covered many thousands of miles by both train and car visiting station sites, and on summer holidays 1,700 miles in 10 days was about average. Petrol, then, was about 5s 0d (25p) a gallon! In every 10 stations visited, one could expect to find nine intact even if the track had been lifted. Gradually that figure dropped until so few remained that it was no longer economical to tour 'on spec' and only those stations known to possess something of interest were visited. The author's photographs reproduced here, cover the whole of that period, the most recent having been taken in 1979. However, I have made a conscious effort to avoid 'modern' signware and blue rolling stock wherever possible, not only because I don't much like it, but also as an incentive to search out older material to illustrate as much as possible of the details, and the little characteristic accessories which have now gone. In order to illustrate some

6

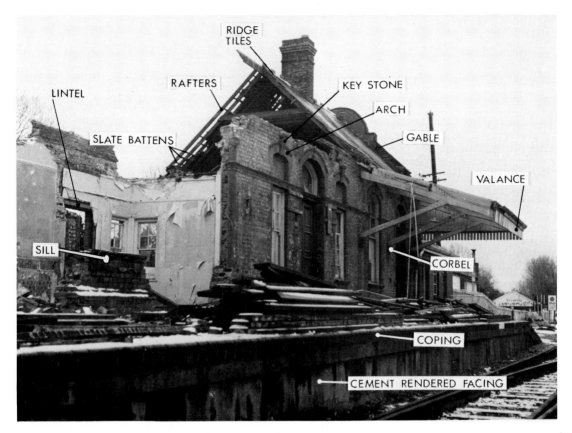

RIDGE TILES

RAFTERS

LINTEL

KEY STONE

ARCH

SLATE BATTENS

GABLE

VALANCE

SILL

CORBEL

COPING

CEMENT RENDERED FACING

Above: The contractors have conveniently 'sectioned' Colnbrook station revealing some of the main structural features in this bleak January, 1979 view. *Author*

Acknowledgements

Special thanks are due to my brother Roger for his company on many of my early outings and for some of the photographs. Similarly to Dr Keith Jaggers whom I met during the closure ceremonies for the Staines branch. To Adrian Knowles for his keen interest in Much Wenlock and for the use of his fine drawing of that station. To N. Caplan, M. Hale, P. H. Wells, R. C. Riley and F. Hornby for the supply of specific prints, and to P. Strong for the loan of his negatives. To Reverend D. Claridge of Tiverton for the loan of negatives and drawings relating to Bampton station, and to Keith Willows for photographs of Badminton and for checking this manuscript. To S. C. Jenkins and H. I. Quayle for material relating to Oxford, Worcester & Wolverhampton line buildings, and to D. Castle for the loan of his 'lion head' negative.

Lastly, to my wife Diane for patience beyond the call of duty while I photographed stations, for holding tape measures and tramping over the ballast of deserted trackbeds. And for pressing me to get on and finish this book.

items, notably the 'backs' of structures, it has been necessary to include some prints which may be a little below standard.

I hope that through my memories of these stations, a little of their character will be evident to the reader, and that I may be forgiven for going into more detail about those stations which were particular favourites.

Introduction

In 1964 it was possible to board the northbound 'Pines Express' at Reading West just after midday and be in Oxford in plenty of time to have a look round before the departure of the 13.25 'stopper' to Worcester. There was the bonus of riding behind a rebuilt Bulleid Pacific over the WR to Oxford, and the choice of leaving the train there, or continuing to Banbury or Leamington with the hope that Oxford shed would turn out one of their grimy 'Castles' for this leg of the journey. I did go on to Leamington on several occasions, but my best memories are of that curious 13.25 (SO) working which survived to be the last steam worked passenger train out of Oxford.

It usually consisted of a couple of Hawksworth coaches and the odd van rattling along behind a 'Grange' or 'Hall' 4-6-0 and stopping at all stations to Evesham, then Pershore and Worcester. On one particularly warm and lazy summer afternoon steam wafted gently upwards from a leaking hose, and some suspension component on the bogie clanked loudly as we came to a halt. 'Anboro, Anboro, this 'ere's Anboro' called the porter as he checked the two coaches for alighting passengers. There weren't any. We left the old station with its shabby brown paintwork basking in the sun amid a blaze of flowers, and rattled and clanked our way through Combe and Finstock, Charlbury, Ascott and Kingham behind No 6868 *Penrhos Grange*, before being deposited at Moreton-in-Marsh.

Here the train set back into a siding and waited for 55 minutes to allow the 13.15 Paddington-Hereford to overtake it. While we examined the many fascinations of Moreton-in-Marsh station, with its grounded coach bodies, and the remains of the old branch to Shipston-on-Stour, the Hereford train came and went behind a 'Hymek' diesel. In the up direction, a Brush Type 4 appeared on a crew-training run at the head of a rake of condemned ex-GWR coaches — ominous forebodings of things to come. Eventually *Penrhos Grange* re-appeared wheezing and gurgling in distinctive fashion and we set off for Chipping Campden to take a last look at the doomed station there.

The goods shed had already gone, but we made careful study of the station buildings. When I returned some years later to give the signalbox similar coverage, the station had gone completely, and last year I found the level crossing replaced by lifting barriers, the signalbox gone and only the row of poplar

trees and the footings of the goods shed to mark this once-attractive station site.

Architecture needs to be uplifting. People, and not least railway passengers I am sure, find the sympathetic soft lines of mature, solid and familiar structures preferable to today's utilitarian and uncompromising approach. Complex rooflines punctuated by chimney stacks and executed in mellowed slates and mossy tiles, for instance, provide a softer, more gentle environment than brash and strident concrete slabs with square corners and a straight skyline. Of course, for commercial properties like railway stations, traditional building materials and styles are simply too expensive for the builders of today's stations. It is all the more sad then, that when

we had such buildings in abundance they were swept away in such a short space of time. The thousands who today pour into St Ives by train can surely find little comfort in the basic facilities which have now been provided in place of the rugged Cornish granite structure which was so in keeping with its surroundings.

As you stand and shiver in a draughty glass shelter or an oversize concrete 'coal bunker' at Drayton Green, or Aldermaston, Handborough, Kings Sutton or Looe it is little comfort to remember that these stations were once all different, with a style and character of their own.

Chris Leigh
Old Windsor 1980

Above: Lustleigh, Devon, in May 1939 shows how a perfect setting and lovely gardens could transform an otherwise rather plain little station to harmonise with its surroundings.
Richard Gee

The Country Station

At the time of the Beeching Report, the quota of country stations on the Western Region was substantially intact. The number of closures each year had been slowly gathering momentum since the early 1950s but these had been generally confined to branches and short sections of line which could be closed completely. Wayside stations on main lines had largely survived unscathed, although pick-up goods services had begun to contract and caused the abandonment of some country goods sheds. There had been a few notable passenger service withdrawals such as the Lambourn Valley and Fairford branches, both of which retained a freight service over part of their length. Some lines in mid-Wales and the West Country had also closed in the early 1960s, but the Beeching Report added the impetus which saw virtually all the small country stations closed or converted to unstaffed bare platforms by 1970.

Many people mourned their passing but often it was impossible to argue with the logic. Deserted platforms and infrequent services told their own tale. The illustration of an up train arriving at Adlestrop, reproduced elsewhere in this book is a typical example. Who could argue for the retention of service where there is clearly no demand? Yet, in some ways it was a 'chicken and egg' situation. Had the poor, often badly

Above: On a damp evening in September 1956, the 21.22 auto-train to Stourbridge Junction waits at Stourbridge Town station. The canopy, with its arcade of columns and ironwork is remarkable, but the platform surface of engineers' blues has been patched with slabs and concrete. *M. A. Walker*

timed, services driven away the traffic, or had the lack of traffic resulted in a gradual reduction of services to a ludicrous level? Clearly the argument will continue for many more years, perhaps until the TUCC reports on individual stations can be made public after the 30-year embargo rule.

Some stations or lines survived Beeching, usually because an alternative bus service would have been impossible, or prohibitively expensive. On the Oxford-Worcester line, Handborough, Combe, Finstock, Ascott and Shipton escaped, but their service was reduced to two up trains and one down train per day. They were quickly reduced to 'basic' status — a weed-grown platform with minimal shelter. The St Ives and Looe branches escaped, largely because the areas they served might be cut-off from road access during severe weather. A dmu driver on the St Ives line once told me that when the salt spray froze to the rails during a bad winter it had taken nearly two hours to climb the steep bank out of the station.

Some service withdrawals were certainly contentious, though, and the Gloucester-Chalford railmotor service was surely high on any such list. The service was quite frequent, and the area it served was well populated, yet it ended in 1964.

The oldest GWR country stations existing at this time were those where some of the structures dated from the days of the broad gauge. Although some retained a number of original buildings, others had been modernised or expanded over the years and incorporated additions from several different dates. In most cases the signalboxes were of standard GWR pattern and dated from around the turn of the century when track layouts were expanded or previous signalling arrangements were modernised.

The hub of the typical country station was the main station building, varying in size according to the importance of the town or village it served, and accordingly, in the accommodation it provided. The most basic consisted of a booking office, waiting room, and an office for the ticket clerk. In such small premises there might well be only one man, dealing with all aspects of the passenger operation. In most places there were facilities for the despatch of parcels and smalls traffic from an office in the station building. The clerk here would deal with all traffic despatched and received by passenger train, and this would include local produce in small quantities, and small amounts of perishables such as rabbits or fowl, perhaps destined for a hotel in one of the larger cities.

Many of the smaller buildings remained oil or gas lit until the end, and some such as the famed Adlestrop were devoid of platform lighting save for a couple of hooks for 'tilley' lamps. The slightly sweet smell of the burning oil and the dim light from the clerk's side of the little ticket window would be familiar to all who had to catch the early morning train to town. There would be too, all the trappings of Great Westernry, the cast signs and wooden bench seats, and perhaps the whole building would remain in the weathered light and dark stone colours which the GWR used for its buildings. The Western Region, of course, adopted the chocolate and cream colour scheme for woodwork on buildings and the date of painting was often shown on the canopy. On interiors a dark battleship grey was often used. Even so, many buildings were never repainted in 15 or more years of BR ownership.

Signalboxes were maintained at the behest of the Signal & Telegraph Department and often received a repaint when the station did not. Some smaller stations would have a signalman/porter whose duties would

include opening the box in the morning perhaps, and signalling the first trains before the signalman came on duty. He then went on to station duties and might be joined by other station staff, although at remote spots such as Rushbury on the Much Wenlock-Craven Arms line a signalman/porter was the only member of staff employed.

By the 1960s many goods sheds were in bad repair due to neglect, or had been closed to traffic. As large numbers of them were built of timber or had a large amount of timber in the roof structure, they disappeared from the scene quickly as goods services were centred on major towns. The passing of many escaped notice altogether, and yet in some cases they were original structures dating from the earliest days of the railway. The typical goods shed had covered accommodation for three or four wagons, an internal platform and a loading bay for road vehicles. An office — often in the form of a lean-to — was provided for the goods clerk or checker, and a timber derrick, hoist, or block and tackle arrangement was provided for lifting heavy loads. Outside, according to the traffic of the district, a hand-operated crane of around six tons capacity might be provided, and also a cattle dock. It is interesting to note that where female staff were employed at the station their duties could involve heavy handling work. The lady clerk at Colnbrook, for instance, recalled just how difficult it was to operate the six ton crane in that goods yard. Today's liberationists might well have paled at the thought!

The goods shed was the collection and distribution centre for local businesses, and worked in conjunction with a parcels delivery service. Horse-drawn parcel vans were in use until displaced by motor lorries during the 1930s and 1940s. The horses were often provided with stables in the goods yard. Those at Staines survived until 1963, and from World War 1 until well into the 1920s had provided a home for *Prince*, who with Carman Drewitt at the reins was a familiar sight in the town. The vans would operate a regular daily round, calling to deliver or pick up from local businesses. Many yards contained a weighbridge, used for weighing road vehicles when heavy lorries were despatched from the yard. The provision and maintenance of the weighbridges was contracted out to H. Pooley & Son, and their 'Weighing machine adjusting van' was occasionally to be seen in a siding or being conveyed in a local freight train. Interestingly, the steel weighing platforms carried the makers details and date on them, and the actual weighing machinery was usually housed in a standard GWR office.

The public duties of the station staff in ticket issuing and handling passenger trains were really only the tip of the iceberg, and the day to day routine included many operations which the public neither saw nor thought about. At a station with, perhaps only one or

Above: The lovely old Cambrian Railways station at Three Cocks Junction seen on 28 July 1959 with a Builth Road-Brecon train on the left and an arrival from Hereford on the right. Note the low platforms. Three Cocks (named after a nearby hostelry) was an interchange with little local traffic and on one occasion at about this time, ticket sales for the day amounted to just 9d (4p). *R. O. Tuck*

Below: Typical of country branch stations in the early 1960s is this view of Leigh Court with its standard GWR nameboard prominent in the foreground. A Gloucester single-unit railcar drops off a few passengers in the final week of Worcester-Bromyard services. *Andrew Muckley*

Below right: The author's favourite train, the 13.25 from Oxford, stands at Moreton-in-Marsh with 'Grange' No 6868 *Penrhos Grange* in charge of two Hawksworth coaches. *R. J. Leigh*

two staff, this could keep them fully occupied. The number and details of every ticket issued were logged, and collected tickets had to be parcelled up with the appropriate form and forwarded to the divisional office. A multitude of diversified stores was used at the station and all these items needed to be re-ordered from time to time. The Great Western was a thrifty company and all stores had to be ordered from Swindon. In many instances items such as a new broom might require return of the old one, as proof of the need! Items of laundry such as towels were sent to Swindon, as were lamps, barrows or furniture requiring repairs. At some stations and yards bicycles were provided for staff and there were strict instructions that these be kept under lock and key when not in use. While staff were entrusted to carry out puncture repairs, cleaning and adjustments, any repairs costing up to 25s 0d (£1.25) could be authorised by a stationmaster. Anything more expensive had to be advised to the Supplies & Contracts Manager, from whom repair kits, lamps and bells were available, provided, of course, that the defective item was returned!

Some larger stations were visited regularly by a stores van, from which 'Tilley' lamps and spare parts could be obtained. Facilities for servicing and lighting of lamps were provided in a separate shed or outbuilding, and if possible this was placed some distance from the other structures because of the risk of fire.

Safety was a prime consideration for station staff, and the rules were explicit in covering every aspect from not slamming carriage doors on passengers' hands, to white lining platform edges. The latter was designed to show the platform edge clearly after dark, and accordingly was not to be applied more than one foot down the ramps at platform ends. Nevertheless, many over-zealous porters painted to the foot of the ramp. Footbridges were always a source of danger. My brother was a victim of the wooden steps at Chalford on a very damp morning in the spring of 1964, before the staff had a chance to put down sand on the steps! On another occasion first aid was required at Kingham when a broken heel sent a lady passenger tumbling down the footbridge steps. Many country stations had only board crossings, and the rule book requested staff to exercise the fullest possible supervision over passengers using these.

Despite the workload, staff at many stations found time to keep elaborate station gardens in order, and indeed, these enhanced the already attractive settings with spectacular effect. It might be flower beds, or a regimented row of evergreens, much loved of the GWR, or, as at Henley-in-Arden, a fine growth of cabbages, with runner beans growing up strings hung from the nameboards. Where the station also included living accommodation there was a further incentive for gardening, and Much Wenlock was noted for a splendid rock garden opposite the platform. The fine clematis which still grows on the MSWJR building at Savernake has several close relatives in Surrey, all grown from a tiny twig once removed on a visit there!

The Brunel Types

To trace the development of the country station one must go back to the very dawn of the Great Western and to its masterful engineer, Isambard Brunel. Here was a man at 28 years old, entrusted with the design of the longest railway then conceived, and who had promised it would be 'the finest work in England'. His railway was designed primarily for passengers and he saw it eventually as part of a through route from London to New York. In order to attract passengers it was necessary that the railway should convey the best possible impression to intending travellers, and this meant that the stations must be designed to please them. The early designs therefore followed the best in traditional styling, were in most cases perfectly matched to their surroundings, and provided sound, comfortable accommodation.

It is not certain exactly which stations Brunel designed, but it is clear that in those early days he laid down certain basic styles, which were then copied or adapted to suit specific locations. The designs which are here attributed to him are instances where the style and detailing are clearly his, although he may not have drawn up the final design for the particular building.

The structures which sprung up in the Thames Valley across Berkshire were neat little red brick buildings following Elizabethan styling and known by Brunel as 'roadside' stations. Stonework was much in evidence for the plinth, quoins and window openings, while the steeply pitched roof was adorned with one of the ornate chimney designs which were a Brunel hallmark. The roofs were of grey slates, and the awning covered all sides. These awnings were one of several Brunel designs, all of which avoided the use of supporting pillars and glass. Stout timber beams were laid across the top of the walls, with their projecting ends carried on decorative cast iron brackets. The awning was

14

constructed on the beams and dropped away from the roof eaves with a gentle slope. Its underside was panelled with tongued and grooved boards, and the top was covered with ridged metal sheets (probably lead).

These are the buildings which featured in several of the Bourne prints, some being swept away when quadrupling took place on the main line. Minety & Ashton Keynes, on the Swindon-Gloucester line survived in original form until the mid-1960s, but today only one neglected example exists, at Culham. In recent years the piecemeal demolition of waiting shelter and goods shed has served to detract from the effectiveness of Culham as a Brunellian survivor, for these buildings were also original and in matching style. As the Great Western system spread, so the design was adapted to suit local conditions and materials. The Culham design, for instance, re-appears in stone and with detail alterations at Brimscombe, a once important point on the Gloucester line. Here a larger waiting shelter was provided on the down platform, and a single road engine shed housed the banker for the climb through the Golden Valley to Sapperton. The station was served by the Gloucester-Chalford local service which was the proving ground for the first GWR steam railmotors and eventually became one of the last strongholds of the '14xx' 0-4-2T and auto-trailer. Services were withdrawn in November 1964, and rather curiously, the footbridge and signalbox outlived the rest of the station by several years.

The same pattern of detailing was used at Melksham and Bradford-on-Avon where the buildings were larger, and built of local stone. Another example, at Shrivenham, lacked the steeply pitched roof but otherwise followed the same style, and despite inclusion on a list of notable buildings prepared by the Victorian Society, it was pulled down in the late 1960s. On my last visit to Melksham the buildings still existed but were derelict. Nearby, Bradford-on-Avon has been cleaned and is quite smart. If one can ignore the shoddy modern signs and truncated chimneys, this is a fine building and even the modernised and reduced canopies have not quite spoiled it.

The second familiar Brunel type was entirely different and followed the Italian Classical style, becoming popularly known as the 'chalet' type. Again, the floor plan consisted of three parts, but this time the roof was a shallow, hipped arrangement with an overhang which formed the awning on all sides. The semi-circular arched windows were in groups of three and the door openings had similar arches. Stonework was much less heavy, but a thin fillet at the base of the arches provided decoration. This 'chalet' style was evidently a favourite of the engineer, for it appears widely throughout his spheres of influence. Part of the

now derelict Chepstow station is in this style, so too are Bridgend, Mortimer on the Reading-Basingstoke line, and the former South Devon Railway buildings at Menheniot. Although this design was usually executed in brick, there were some timber examples, a notable survivor being Charlbury on the Oxford, Worcester & Wolverhampton line. To simplify the construction, the groups of windows are, in this case, replaced by a single round topped window.

The building at Hatch is a good example of the development of this style. It is constructed of red brick and incorporates the simplified window shape used at Charlbury, with its obvious advantages in admitting light. The roof overhang, however, was reduced to being decorative rather than functional, and instead of the shaped timber beams, the Victorian cast iron brackets were used.

At Chard this design is tied to another Brunel hallmark, the overall train-shed, which is probably his most well-known station feature. The earliest of these train-sheds appeared at the 'one-sided' stations such as Slough and Reading. These curios had both up and down platforms on the same side of the line, and were really two stations, each with independent facilities. As these occurred at major towns they are outside the scope of this book and are mentioned only because their train-sheds were the forerunners of several small country stations. The most well-loved of these were Moretonhampstead and Ashburton in Devon. These two are best dealt with as twins, for they had similar stone offices attached to the austere timber barn.

The train-sheds were intended to provide an added degree of luxury for passengers, permitting them to pass from the waiting room to the train with minimum exposure to the elements. In practice, due to the relatively low roof, they were smoke traps, and those pictures which show them in later years depict all too well the dingy and rather spartan interiors. The last of the main line examples, at Totnes, was rebuilt during the 1930s but the branch examples survived until their respective routes were closed. The goods sheds at both Ashburton and Moretonhampstead were stone-built to match the station offices, and thus presented a more substantial appearance than the train-sheds.

At Chard Central the Italianate station offices were tied to an overall train-shed of brick construction, with an arched wall and 'Classical' gable ends. It resembled the entrance to an Egyptian temple without the supporting columns. This was a larger structure than usual, and another on this scale existed at Thame, although with much plainer offices. The station at Ashburton was preserved for a short time by the Dart Valley Railway, until a road improvement scheme severed it from their system, and it was sold to a local trader. The Brunel styling was closely followed by Hannaford in his design for Frome, to the extent that it

is often attributed to Brunel. It is now the only survivor of the small train-shed type still in use on the WR. Unfortunately, as is so often the case with smaller stations of architectural interest, it is considered too large for present requirements. As a result of neglect in recent years, and 'rationalisation', it is in a sorry state and unlikely to warrant adequate repairs, although it was expected to receive attention during 1980.

Other Brunel stations are more difficult to categorise and are really instances of the use of standard features in an individualistic building. At Cirencester, for instance, Brunel produced a building to suit the important Roman city. It originally had a

train-shed, but over the years piecemeal alterations have left only a curiously tall segment of the original building which has something of a Hammer horror-movie set about its appearance. Above the modern canopy a fine bay window survives, with a stone scroll which has never received its inscription. In the 1970s it served as a bus station, but its long-term future even in this role is doubtful, despite inclusion on the Department of Environment list of historic buildings.

At Stonehouse Brunel produced a rather spartan stone design which, like many of his structures, had its ornate chimneys removed in later years. However, it was redeemed by the matching shelter on the up platform which retained its fine chimney to the end. The down platform was lower than normal, and remained so until rebuilding occurred in 1976. The reconstruction was opposed and the buildings were listed by the Department of Environment. However the BR authorities were unwilling to maintain them and applied for permission to close the station. In order to retain the passenger service, consent to the demolition was given, and the present Stonehouse buildings are noteless stone boxes.

All the surviving Brunel structures are worthy of retention, but the future of several, particularly the Starcross pumping house and the original Temple Meads (likely to become a Brunel museum), remains uncertain at the time of writing.

Left: Bradford-on-Avon follows the same Elizabethan styling as the 'roadside' stations. Truncated chimneys and canopies, and modern signware have not quite spoiled it. *Author*

Below left: The road side of Bradford-on-Avon. Note the treatment of gable ends, the bars on the booking office window, the railings and gate posts. *Les Bertram*

Below: This 1961 view of Brimscombe shows clearly the ridged roofing material used on the awnings. The valancing and the facing of the bay window are not typical but the wooden paling fence and blue enamel nameboard are early GWR details. *M. J. Esau*

Left: Beyond the standard plate girder footbridge stands an original Brunel era goods shed. The station buildings have been updated and the lamp posts are examples of 1950s modernisation. Melksham on 4 January, 1965. *G. R. Hounsell*

Below left: The up platform shelter at Stonehouse seen shortly before demolition. Note the Brunel chimney. *Author*

Right: Cirencester Town has been much modified to serve as a bus station, but the upper bay window is still particularly fine. *Author*

Below: A question mark still hangs over the future of Brunel's atmospheric railway pumping house at Starcross. This remarkable piece of Italianate Victorian architecture housed the steam pumping engine, and the tower which was once topped with a campanile, disguised the chimney. *T. W. Nicholls*

BRUNEL 'CHALET' DESIGNS

The two most distinctive Brunelian designs for small stations were the 'Elizabethan' roadside type and the Italianate 'chalets'. In the latter category there are two excellent survivors, Mortimer and Charlbury. The station at Mortimer is particularly important as it has survived largely unaltered in its external aspects and it has also retained its matching waiting shelter. Both structures are built of brick in Flemish bond and represent the style in its most perfect form. The decoration has been kept simple and consists only of some relief brickwork and elegantly shaped beams under the overhanging roof. The degree of symmetry is remarkable, even to the extent of one or two 'blind' arches to match doors or windows.

The drawings illustrate both up and down platform buildings at Mortimer as they were when measured in 1979. At this time the station was boarded up and in a poor state of repair, with only the main doorway on the platform side left open to enable passengers to shelter from the elements. Vandalism had inevitably taken its toll, and with so much of the structure inaccessible it has not been possible to prepare an interior ground plan.

The smaller building was never anything more than a shelter, and there was no public access to the two enclosed areas with their 'blind' arches. A boarded area at the back of one of these suggests that there might at some stage have been a doorway to enable it to serve as a store shed.

Both sides of the main structure are identical, except that the two cast iron hoppers and down pipes are to be found only on the road side. Hence, I have shown only one elevation. The ends, however, differed as shown. Unlike the waiting shelter, which has cast iron 'ogee' guttering, the main structure has an integral gutter, shown sectioned in black in one end elevation. It consists of a timber trough lined with lead sheet. The underside of the roof overhang on both buildings is lined with 6in tongue-and-groove boards.

At the time of writing it is understood that Mortimer is scheduled for cleaning and renovation, and that the booking hall will be returned to its original use, with the provision of a full time member of staff in attendance. Passenger traffic from the station appears to be quite encouraging and there is certainly every justification for ensuring the future of this attractive and architecturally important station.

A few miles from Mortimer, on the nearby Berks & Hants main line, the stations at Theale and Aldermaston were also Brunel chalets. Both were almost identical to the Mortimer building, while at Aldermaston the down platform shelter was indeed an exact replica of the Mortimer type. This shelter outlasted the main building by a few years, but it has now been replaced by a steel-framed glass shelter. Other examples appeared on the South Devon Railway, at Ivybridge for instance, and at Menheniot where the building suffered from later alterations and a cement-rendered finish.

Charlbury is an interesting example of the chalet type built almost entirely of wood. A similar structure at Evesham was replaced by a GWR standard station late in the last century. These two may have been built of timber in the interests of economy, or possibly because of the influence of John Fowler, who took over from Brunel as civil engineer before construction of the buildings commenced. The windows were reduced to a single arch to simplify construction, the dimensions are reduced, and at Charlbury, the accommodation has been increased with a brick-built rear extension.

The down platform was extended and provided with a new, but very basic, corrugated iron waiting shelter by the GWR. This replaced a rather attractive timber shelter similar to the one at Chipping Campden. The lengthening of the platform also accounts for the rather curious position of the water tank, which ended up halfway along the platform, having originally been at the western end. The existence of goods yard sidings at both ends prevented lengthening of the up platform and long trains were required to draw up twice. After the goods yard was closed and the sidings removed, local conservationists, for reasons best known to themselves, resisted a move by BR to lengthen the platform. Thus, passengers for Charlbury are nowadays requested to travel in the front three coaches only.

In recent years, in spite of improved services, the track at Charlbury has been singled and the former down line removed. At the same time the station was treated to the Western Region's ultimate in uninspired paint schemes — pale grey with 'forget-me-not' blue trim. This particular treatment (probably due to lack of adequate surface preparation) always seems to have weathered badly and been prone to exceptional attacks of peeling. It looked shabby very quickly indeed.

The station received a major facelift in 1979 and gained national recognition when local commuters campaigned against the installation of an electric fire

Above right: Theale station was a standard Brunel 'chalet'. In this 1963 view it shows signs of a major structural fault, with the nearer end supported by heavy timber buttresses. Note the barred windows and the wooden broad-gauge era goods shed. *Michael Hale*

Right: The down platform shelter at Aldermaston was the standard type designed to match the chalets. *K. A. Jaggers*

Photo Survey : MORTIMER

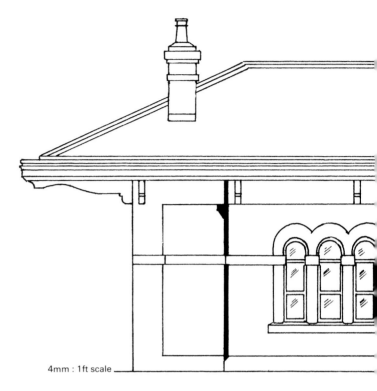

4mm : 1ft scale

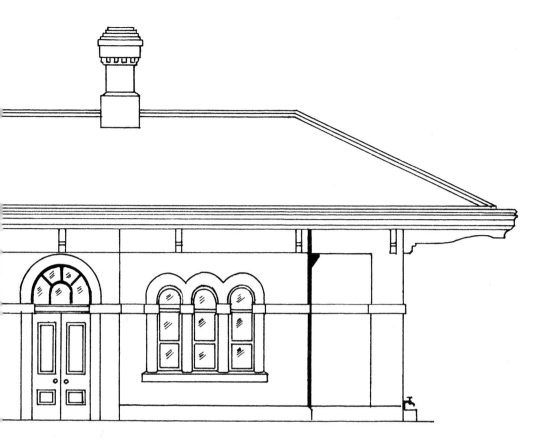

Above: Mortimer, east elevation.

Left: The Brunel chalet at Mortimer seen in 1979. *Author*

in the waiting room. The campaign HOOF (Hands off our fire) ensured the retention of the cosy coal fires in the ticket hall and waiting room despite the reconstruction of much of the station interior. The modernisation is bright and tasteful, although sadly the traditional ticket window has gone, and it has been achieved despite considerable difficulties. The structure was found to be in a poor state and much of the woodwork required replacement.

Externally, little has changed, but the colour scheme is now an attractive combination of pastel fawn and brown, not unlike 'modern' versions of the GWR stone shades. The window frames are white and the eaves, fitted with inconspicuous flourescent lighting, are picked out in red. The treatment of this structure marks a major advance in the fortunes of the few remaining examples of good architecture on the Western Region. To cap it all, at the time of my last visit there had been no outbreak of corporate image sign-ware, and a restored GWR nameboard with cast iron posts had appeared at the Oxford end of the platform. Previously, as in GWR practice there had been a large nameboard only at the approach (Evesham) end of the up platform.

23

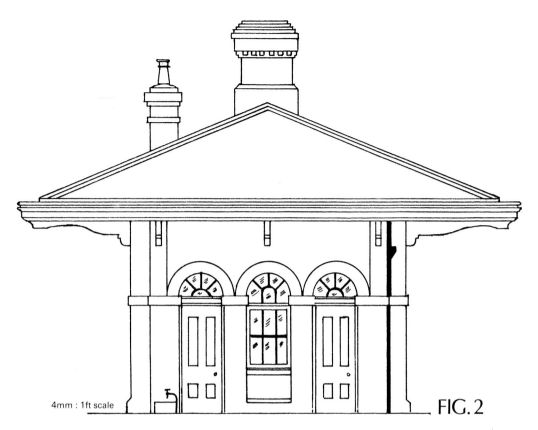

4mm : 1ft scale

FIG. 2

24

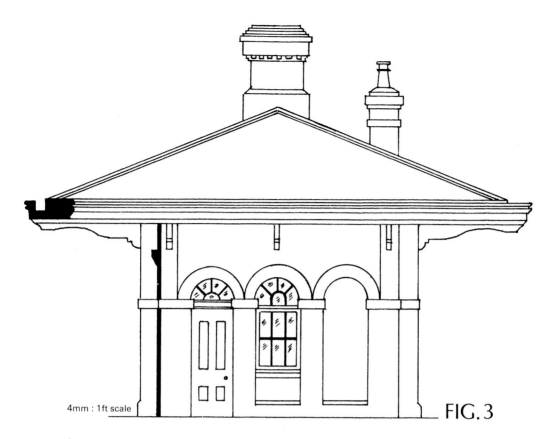

4mm : 1ft scale

FIG. 3

Above left: Mortimer, north elevation.

Above: Mortimer, south elevation.

Left: Mortimer seen from the station yard showing clearly the arches and shaped beams, and a row of dentils around the main chimney stack. *Author*

Right: Detail under the awning at Mortimer. *Author*

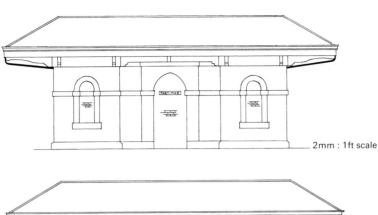

2mm : 1ft scale

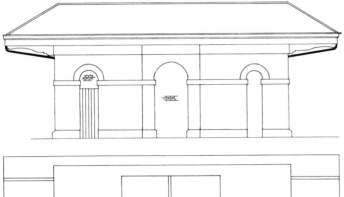

Left: Mortimer waiting shelter.

Below: The Brunel chalet as interpreted by Fowler for the Oxford, Worcester & Wolverhampton Railway. Charlbury in unbecoming BR grey, when renovation had just begun. *Author*

Right: Charlbury looking fresh and splendid after tasteful renovation. Compare this photograph with the similar view of Mortimer and note differences in boarding and gutters. *Author*

Above: The approaching passenger's view of Chard Central. The treatment of gables on office and train shed is interesting. The chimneys appear to have suffered from rebuilding. *R. C. Riley*

Below: An unusual view inside the train-shed at Tavistock South with an auto-train waiting to leave for Plymouth. *J. H. Aston*

Two views of Frome station in 1978. Hannaford's train-shed has been propped up at one end and the surroundings are untidy. Note the late GWR era concrete lamp posts — similar to those used by the Southern Railway. *Both Author*

Early Standard Types

The designs which Brunel produced for the station at Box provided the starting point for another standardised style which was in vogue during the 1850s. These are perhaps the closest that the GWR ever came to reflecting the Victorian love of over-decoration in any of its 'standard' designs. They were single-storey structures, larger than the 'roadside' types, and provided substantial station offices but no dwelling accommodation. The surviving examples were all constructed from local stone. The main identifying features were a recessed section on the platform side, a small but heavily constructed porch over the booking office entrance, and a substantial awning around all the walls.

The supporting canopy brackets were now more substantial than those of Brunel, the awning was carried on steel girders and was fitted with decorative wooden valancing. Where the girders pierced the valancing they were capped with a curious Victorian gargoyle in the form of a lion's mask. This was a two-part casting consisting of the lion's head which filled the depth of the valancing, surmounted by a separate crown piece which rose above the awning. The accompanying illustration shows the main casting only. The original came from Heyford and with its paintwork restored shows the detail remarkably well.

Above: Aynho for Deddington, a solidly Victorian design in mellow local stone. Although now a coal office, the view from the station approach has changed little. *Author*

Right: Heyford station has managed to remain attractive despite the loss of its canopy. In this 1979 view it still wears GWR light and dark stone paintwork more than 20 years old! *Author*

The origin of these beasts is obscure but it is likely that the castings and possibly even the original patterns were made at Swindon. Note that the beast's face, variously described as a lion or a leopard, has human eyes.

In GWR days the valancing was painted in light stone, with the trim boards and 'masks' in dark stone. The decorative ironwork so beloved of the Victorians was to see only one more interpretation in GWR small station design before the advent of structural steelwork.

It is doubtful whether timber valancing had ever figured in any of Brunel's original designs, although in later interpretations and during refurbishing it was added to some. At Grange Court there was a good example of the lion's mask type without valancing, but the result was austere and unappealing. The design looked its best as it appeared at Kidlington, Aynho and Heyford, and also at Clynderwen in Wales. The buildings on the Oxford-Aynho section, just mentioned, were virtually identical, and all still exist. By a combination of fate, and presumably some enterprising work at local level, all three have now been let and are privately occupied.

They are built of local stone, in a random bond, with much decoration in dressed stone blocks. This decoration includes quoins, windows, sills and the porch. The waiting room at the Oxford end of each building has a neat stone-built bay window.

Aynho now serves as the local coal office for Charringtons, with its platform removed, the canopy cut back and the recess area bricked up. It has been partly repainted in blue and grey, and apart from the addition of a small weigh-house to one of the windows, the road elevation looks much as it always has done. The up platform has largely disappeared, and with it the matching waiting shelter with its two tiny rooms and roof-mounted water tanks. The visitor should not miss the pretty cottage provided for the stationmaster. It is to the same design as the one at Adlestrop and its lovely country garden retains a gate to the non-existant platform.

The condition of Kidlington is similar to Aynho and it is let to a local business, the whole of its station yard now being covered by a sprawl of small business premises. It is painted in green and black and the porch still retains a couple of the lion masks, though the crowns are missing.

Above: A lion mask from Heyford station showing the curious detailing of this cast iron decoration. A 'crown' casting was attached to the top bolt hole. *D. Castle*

Photo Survey : HEYFORD

The position of Heyford is a little different from that of its neighbours, for the station remains open to passengers. Nevertheless, the building stood derelict for a while during 1978/9 and its passenger accommodation was replaced by the inevitable glass shelter. The station is nicely sited on a curve with the canal close by, and it retains a lattice footbridge, until recently finished in GWR dark stone paint.

The building here has lost its canopy completely but the structure has been made good so that the loss is not too obvious. It is likely that the north end of the structure was extended at some time. There is a tell-tale line of quoins at the join, and the newer windows are of marginally different dimensions.

The accompanying drawings are in effect a composite, taken from site measurements of Heyford in 1979 but with the canopy details added to one end elevation and part of the road elevation. These are based on the canopy at Aynho. Note that the platform level is higher than the station yard and all doorways off the platform therefore have two shallow steps down. The return wall 'A' is shown in Detail A, while that at 'B' is a mirror image of 'A'. The two blind apertures in the recess are infilled with matching stonework and do not appear to have ever been windows. The drawing shows one lion mask and crown only for reference but these occurred at the intersection of the valancing with each canopy bracket. Small gaps in the stone fillet below the facia show the positions of the canopy brackets. Fig 6 shows the shape of the canopy in relation to the ground plan of the building. The north end of the structure is shown in Fig 3, with Fig 4 showing the same elevation with the covered screen in place. Note that the three chimneys may have been rebuilt. Originally they were probably similar to the Brunel chimney shown in the photograph of Kidlington.

Throughout its career as a station Heyford retained its light and dark stone paintwork. During 1979 it was let to a firm of motor parts factors and has since been repainted in a rather unbecoming orange and lime green. The station remains open largely to serve the nearby Upper Heyford base of the US Air Force.

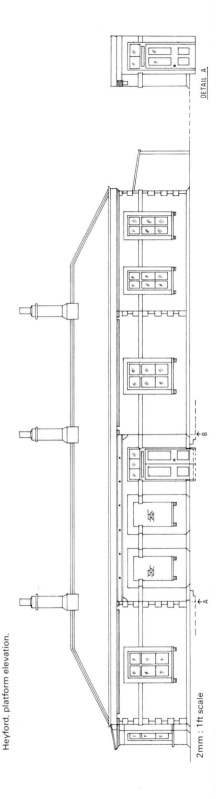

Heyford, platform elevation.

DETAIL A

B

A

2mm : 1ft scale

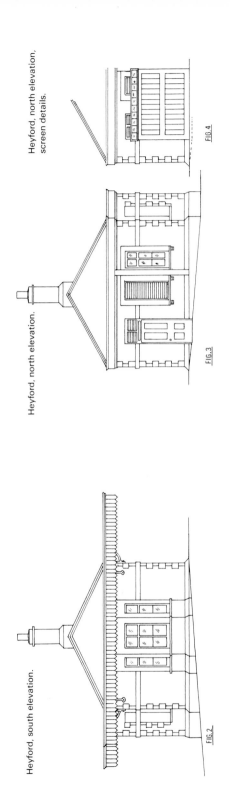

Heyford, north elevation,
screen details.

FIG.4

Heyford, north elevation.

FIG.3

Heyford, south elevation.

FIG.2

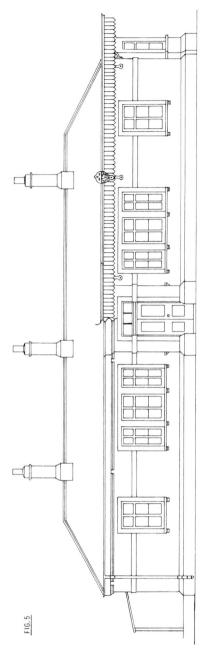

FIG.5

Heyford, west elevation.

33

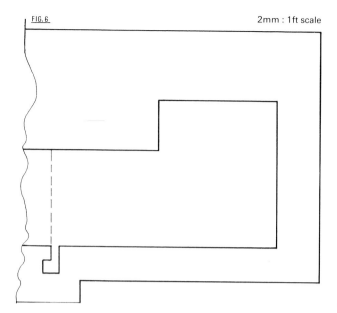

FIG. 6   2mm : 1ft scale

Left: Heyford, part ground plan.

Right: Detail of the bay window at Heyford. *Author*

Below right: A glimpse inside the booking hall at Heyford, when derelict, looking out towards the porch. Note the thickness of the wall, which necessitates the deeply recessed ticket window. *Author*

Far bottom right: The porch and canopy at Kidlington still retaining two lion masks. Compare the left hand chimney stack with the one at Stonehouse. *Author*

The Italianate style begun by Brunel was developed after his death to produce a later standard style which found limited use. Notable examples were at Marlow now demolished) and Taplow, where the station was designed in 1871, but not built until 1883. The Taplow buildings still exist and are particularly fine, with their rows of window arches producing the effect of a colonnade. Other features of these buildings included an elaborate form of valancing and cast canopy columns in the form of fasces, the Roman symbol of authority, much evident in GWR decoration. It is based on a bunch of rods bound together, and also appears in one of the tunnel portals at Box.

These supporting columns are clearly visible in the lovely night view of Stourbridge Town taken in 1956. The gradual growth of canopies after the Brunel era is evident here. The ironwork brackets, full of intricate fretwork, now form an arch through the length of the peaked canopy roof and the deep timber end valancing is profiled to match the arched shape. The platform is surfaced with the familiar 'engineers blues' but has been patched with concrete and slabs.

At Stourbridge Town, the building itself was an early example of a pattern which became the GWR standard from the later years of the 19th century. It was constructed in cream sanitary bricks with a decoration of reds and with stonework for sills and lintels. Many of these buildings possessed square slated turrets surmounted by an array of decorative wrought ironwork, and as this style spread to some of the larger stations some examples still exist. The Stourbridge structure lost its canopy and was reduced to a sorry state before being replaced by a new station built during 1979. This is sited immediately beyond the

old station platform, thus making this very short branch line even shorter.

At Kingham and Ross-on-Wye the styling was similar, but both examples have now gone and one must turn to larger stations such as West Drayton, where the structure remains, linked to its subterranean passages. The down fast line building at Hanwell & Elthorne was another example, but this has been demolished and the sorry tale of attempted conservation here is perhaps best forgotten, although one hopes that some lessons have been learned.

With this design the GWR achieved what were probably its first structures which were purely railway in style, with no harking back to Elizabethan Gothic or Italian styles. The next stage in the evolution of the country station building disposed of the turrets and ironwork, reduced the small structures to a simple rectangular plan, and provided a self-supporting canopy. Thus in the closing years of the 19th century the railway had evolved a simple standard style that could be easily applied to stations, weighbridge offices, sheds and even stables. The degree of standardisation in buildings was to become as marked as that in locomotive practice. The economies which could be achieved by the use of standard, factory-produced joinery for doors and window frames, and the ease with which modification and extension could be carried out will be self-evident.

Shipton for Burford

Shipton station was originally provided with one of the simple wooden station buildings built by the Oxford Worcester & Wolverhampton Railway. The station served the village of Shipton, but was not ideally situated, being some distance from the centre of the village. Rather optimistically it claimed also to serve the much larger village of Burford, known as 'the gateway to the Cotswolds', but this village was several miles beyond Shipton. There is no doubt that in its early years Shipton was a successful station, and by the 1880s traffic had outgrown the available facilities and a new station building was constructed.

The new building was to a standard GWR design in which a series of different 'bays' could be drawn up in a variety of combinations to produce a structure suitable for almost any location. Other examples were at Kingham, Moreton-in-Marsh, Ross-on-Wye and Pershore. The Shipton building was a typical example with five 'bays' and replaced the original building on the up platform. The down platform was provided with a standard waiting shelter. Both structures were built of red brick under a grey slate roof.

The drawings depict the structure as it was in the 1960s after the canopy had been removed, with one side elevation showing the details of the canopy. The

location of the supporting canopy brackets can be seen from the gaps in the projecting brickwork shown on the front elevation and in the photographs. Unfortunately, no details of the rear of the structure have come to light, but this was devoid of canopy and had few, if any, windows. In later years it was substantially obscured by a large lean-to built of pressed concrete sections. All the stone lintels over doors and windows were picked out in cream paint, while the curved arches above them were formed by a course of blue bricks.

For a time Shipton was evidently one of the busier wayside stations on this section of line. The typical black timber goods shed, at the Evesham end of the station on the up side was surrounded by a fairly substantial yard in which a number of supplementary sheds were erected over the years. There were two corrugated iron sheds in the yard, and another smaller one on the up platform. The two larger ones were probably erected in wartime and subsequently taken over for farm feed stores. There was a neat timber goods office behind the main station building, and this and most of the small buildings were still standing in 1979. A stable block of standard design still stands in the goods yard and is unusual in having the floor raised well above ground level. It must at one time have had a wooden ramp at the front to provide access but this has now gone and the building is derelict. The stable was built of red and blue brick under a slate roof. It had a wooden floor and provided stalls for three horses.

Above: A skip of concrete swings above the roof of Taplow station as new platform footings are installed. The unbroken row of arches, and unusual valancing are features of this particular design. *Author*

Right: Two views of Marlow showing its general similarity to Taplow. The tradition of fine chimneys established by Brunel has been continued on this structure. *Ian Allan Library*

At the Oxford end of the station, on the down side, were further sidings serving a substantial feedstuffs mill. This mill is still in production but the rail connection has gone. The signalbox was sited at this end of the station to control the sidings and to give a good view around the long curve on which the station stands.

By the 1960s traffic had declined to the extent that the Shipton goods shed was closed and demolished as pick-up goods services over the line were withdrawn and freight railheads substituted. Only Handborough and Charlbury, of the smaller stations, retained their sheds for a while longer. Soon all the sidings at Shipton were gone, and with them the signalbox, and it was no surprise to find Shipton among the closure proposals in the Beeching Report. The station did not close, however, as it proved impossible to provide a substitute bus service to suit the wayside stations between Oxford and Moreton-in-Marsh.

Shipton was reduced to an unstaffed halt with a service of just three trains per day. The main station building survived in a derelict state until it was replaced by a bus shelter early in 1971.

Above: Stourbridge Town station, seen here in the late 1960s, shows how the size of canopies had increased to the point where supporting columns were required. *Author*

Below: In 1978 the exterior of Stourbridge Town still looked grand despite some sealed doorways and the loss of its canopy. The turrets and ironwork decoration show clearly, as does the pattern of stone lintels and brick arches over the openings. *K. M. Busby*

STOURBRIDGE TOWN

GENTLEMEN

Photo Survey : SHIPTON

Below: Shipton, east elevation.

Bottom: Shipton for Burford had a basic version of the Stourbridge design, but built in red brick and without turrets or ironwork. Its canopy, removed c1960 was supported on brackets. The nameboard is an early BR type with concrete posts having dowel peg holes to accommodate different depths of board. *Michael Hale*

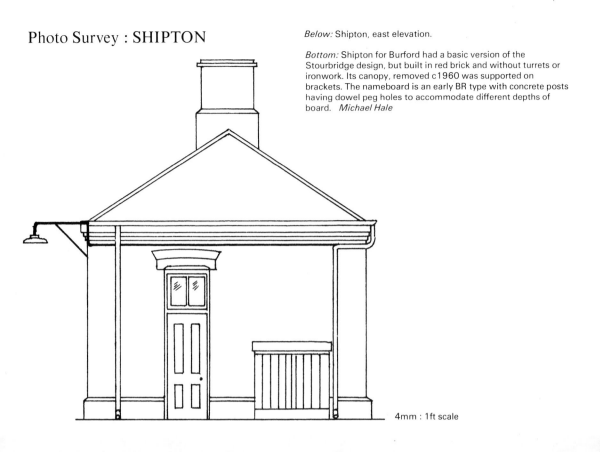

4mm : 1ft scale

4mm : 1ft scale

Above: Shipton, platform elevation.

Left: Shipton, west elevation.

Right: Shipton seen shortly before demolition. The locations of the canopy brackets show clearly, as does the recessed downspout.
Oxfordshire County Museums

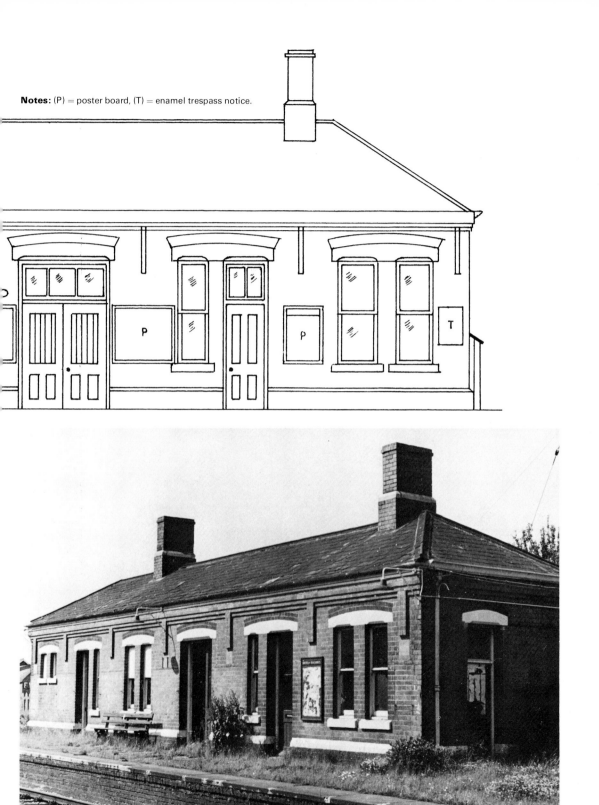

Notes: (P) = poster board, (T) = enamel trespass notice.

Above: A general view of Ross-on-Wye station in 1966 showing a particularly pleasing application of this design. Both buildings are in matching style, and have the luxury of draught screens under the canopies. *N. Caplan*

Below: A glimpse under the canopy at Ross-on-Wye shows its similarity to Stourbridge Town. The profusion of hanging flower baskets and GWR signs make this a real gem. *Ian Allan Library*

20th Century Standard Styles

From 1900 the Great Western entered a period of consolidation but although its main network was now well-established the construction of cut-off routes and the expansion and reconstruction of stations provided ample opportunity for use of the new designs. In many instances the location of new stations can be seen, with benefit of hindsight, to be ill-advised. Frequently, the company provided stations at points where the line passed near a village with little traffic potential, or it might be suggested, because there was a long stretch without a station and it felt that railheads should be provided every few miles. It was this situation which led to the decimation of this style of station structure just before and during the Beeching era, when intermediate stations on lines such as Wootton Basset-Severn Tunnel and the Birmingham line were swept away.

The sheer number of structures produced in this style means that there are a number of good survivors, varying in size from Evesham down to Wargrave on the Henley branch. The normal construction material was deep red bricks with varying amounts of relief in the form of blues for plinth, corners and window apertures. The corner bricks were rounded, being known as 'bullnosed', and the hipped Bangor slate roof was provided with a triangular

Above: Badminton basks in the summer sun in the days when car parking cost 2s 6d (12$\frac{1}{2}$p) per day. This was a perfect example of a standard building, even down to the arrangement of canopy and footbridge. *K. R. Willows*

skylight over the gents' toilet. The standard canopy was cantilevered from the wall on a steel frame made of factory-assembled components. It had a pitched roof which was clad with corrugated iron on the front slope, and 'Invincible' glazing on the rear. These canopies were normally to be found only on the platform side of the building, although some were extended to join the roof of a covered footbridge.

Among the small stations in this style were Mitcheldean Road and Fawley on the Ross line, parts of Llangollen, Wells Tucker Street and Bramley, to name but a few.

This design was also used to supplement existing station facilities, and one such example was Savernake Low Level where the lovely B&H station was originally provided with only a single platform. The GWR used the restricted facilities as an excuse for delaying MSWJR trains which were obliged to use the station until the frustrations caused them to open their independent Savernake-Marlborough section in 1898. In the meantime a Board of Trade inspector insisted

Above: An unusual view of the roof at Badminton showing the canopy covering of corrugated sheets and 'Invincible' glazing. Although originally a hipped roof design, at the far end an extension in the later style has been added. *K. R. Willows*

Below: Tetbury in 1963, with an AC Cars diesel railbus waiting to depart for Kemble. The building followed the standard pattern but re-used joinery, canopy parts and probably roof covering from an earlier timber structure. *Leslie Sandler*

Above: Standard chimney stacks and the triangular skylight over the gents' toilet are prominent in this view of Malvern Wells station being dismantled in 1966. *N. Caplan*

Below: A sorry-looking Badminton in 1976 with its footbridge roof gone, and most doors and windows bricked up. *G. Scott-Lowe*

that the GWR should improve their facilities, and so a down platform was provided in 1883 and the standard pattern buildings erected in 1900 for the opening of the Stert (near Patney)-Westbury line. The drawings accompanying this section depict this design as it was drawn up for buildings at Little Somerford, Coalpit Heath and Badminton on the direct South Wales line.

A modification to this style was adopted in the first years of the 20th century and although the basic rectangular structure remained, the styling of windows was amended and the hipped, slated roof gave way to a flat roof of reinforced concrete. This carried a frame of structural steelwork which formed a canopy over the entire structure. At larger stations such as Lapworth and Tyseley two buildings were placed end to end with a single canopy structure covering both.

This style was used for new stations and reconstructions and a particularly nice example formed the terminus of the Lambourn branch. Here, the original 1898 Lambourn Valley Tramway building was replaced in about 1907 with the new building carried on a series of blue brick arches. It became well-known, as the picturesque branch was always popular with enthusiasts, but was also interesting in that the other LVT buildings at Lambourn including the goods and engine sheds remained in near original condition until closure in 1961. The delightful LVT booking office from Welford Park is now preserved at Didcot Steam Centre.

Above: The flat-roofed building and the steelwork supporting the canopy can be clearly seen in this view of Littlemore. *Author*

Below: Castle Cary station is unusual in having a rugged and individualistic structure to which a standard pattern canopy has been fitted. *Author*

Above: The unique GWR railcar, No W18W is seen arriving at Lambourn on 28 August, 1954. This building replaced the original LVT structure, and the platform was evidently extended at the same time. The join is visible on the platform face, where the shadow commences. *J. W. Rae*

Below: 'The end *is* nigh' at Wootton Bassett on 14 October 1966 as a 'Hymek' rolls by with a down freight. The down platform has already gone. *K. R. Willows*

Above: Uxbridge High Street station looks remarkably ramshackle on 26 September 1954 as streamlined railcar No W13W departs with a London Railway Society tour. *S. C. Nash*

The cut-off lines built in the early years of the present century possessed a number of examples of this turn of the century red brick type, but most have now disappeared. On my last visit the station at Saunderton on the GW&GC Joint section was still standing, and in use, but further down the line the closed stations at Haddenham, Blackthorn and Ardley, all built in this style, had gone. By chance I was returning from a visit to Calne on 2 January 1965 and caught the 18.09 Chippenham-Swindon local, formed of two Hawksworth coaches behind a rather lively 'Hymek'. This was the last train to call at Dauntsey and Wootton Bassett (even this missed Christian Malford Halt, which was closed earlier in the day), and on a poster board on the dimly-lit platform at Wootton were scrawled the immortal words 'The end is nigh, prepare to meet thy bus'. Wootton and the stations to Hullavington have been razed but parts of Badminton and Chipping Sodbury have survived, though hardly intact. One of the buildings at Chipping Sodbury survives minus its canopy, serving as a coal office. Badminton's curious status among the nobility appears to have protected it from demolition, but only the fast lines remain in place, and with its platform roads gone the building has had all its doors and windows bricked up.

Other examples like Shifnal in the West Midlands have lost their canopies and steelwork and remain open only as ugly brutalised boxes. There was a period

when the WR had a mania for despoiling canopies, egged on by the payment of a premium for each one removed. At Littlemore on the Oxford-Princes Risborough branch a good example of this type remained intact, complete with canopy after closure, and was occupied by a local trader, but it has now gone. Perhaps the most remarkable version of this style was situated not at a country station at all, but at Uxbridge High Street. Here, the profile followed the standard style and the structural steelwork was the same, but the building itself, and the platform, were constructed of timber. By 1954 the whole structure was in a dreadful state and must have disappeared soon after.

Mention must also be made of one or two variations which were especially attractive. One such was Tetbury where the frugal Great Western rebuilt the branch termius in 1914. Although standard brickwork was employed and the overall character followed the standard design much of the joinery, windows, doors and roofing material from the original timber structure were re-used. The standard goods shed and engine shed were provided at an earlier date. The window and door arrangement of the station building was most distinctive, as was the roofing in grey slates laid in a diamond pattern like North American shingles. There was a matching lamp hut on the platform and the latter was, in its final years, unlit and overgrown. The branch has been well documented elsewhere and is particularly favoured by modellers.

Chalford was a splendid example of a standard red brick station differing from the normal only in having a narrower canopy. There were other examples similarly provided where the standard canopy was not suitable, notably at Wrangaton and at Henllan in Wales. At Chalford both up and down platform buildings were in matching style and to the end the down side possessed one of those coveted gas lamps with the station name in blue on its opal glass front. The up platform originally had a bay platform at the Kemble end, but this was later fenced off when the platform was lengthened with a 1930s era concrete sectional extension.

Set as it was in a steep sided valley the station reverberated to the thunder of 'Castles' attacking Sapperton bank and had a local service provided by

Below: Cold and uninviting, Iver's 1930s era station is now in Western Region commuter-land. *Kevin Lane*

'14xxs' with auto-trailers. The experience of one of these propelling at near 70mph on the downhill run to Gloucester was not easily forgotten. Chalford was probably as near a perfect GWR station as one could have hoped to find in the early 1960s. Closure came on 2 November 1964 and the site is now a council yard, with only the weighbridge office still standing.

From the World War 1 period the amount of station building and rebuilding declined, and with it the need for such extensive standardisation. As a result a number of 'freak' designs, produced as one-offs or in limited quantities, appeared. The stations at Tettenhall, Wombourn and Himley south of Wolverhampton, were all similar in style and owed much to the standard red brick patterns. The design, however, was more austere and the canopy structure reverted to 19th century practice. The construction of these three stations was really a last remnant of prewar new line building, for construction had begun in 1913 but the line was not opened until 1924. It closed to passengers within eight years, a victim of efficient road competition.

During the mid-1930s the writing must already have been on the wall for many country stations, yet elaborate rebuilding was carried out at both Bourton-on-the-Water and Stow-on-the-Wold in 1936. While

there was some justification for the imposing Cotswold stone structure at Bourton, a flourishing venue for trippers, there can have been very limited potential at Stow, where the station was at the foot of a steep hill some 1½ miles from the village. Both stations were attractively designed to match the local architecture, with thick stone walls and 'leaded light' windows. They were traditional to the point of being old-fashioned and could not really be cited as a development of station architecture, although they were an undoubted improvement in facilities over the structures they replaced. At Bourton, a curious feature was the provision of a folding latticework barrier at the booking office exit, a feature seldom found at country stations. Other doors were in the solid, wood-grained 'Elizabethan' style associated with many private houses erected during the 1930s.

Another odd one-off design was the one drawn up for Blockley in the 1920s to replace the existing OW&W timber building. There was little improvement in the facilities or styling so one must assume that it was the poor state of the original, rather than increasing traffic which prompted the new design. The building was on wooden stilts and its only redeeming feature was a hip-roofed porch on the platform side. I must admit that I took little notice of it during my visits to the line, and can remember it only as a drab structure of almost unrelieved creosote colour. Another undistinguished station of this period was Stoke Canon, the alteration to which resulted from the provision of new running loops there in 1932.

On the other hand, the inter-war station at Iver (first opened in December 1924) is one that I remember only too well, and it was high on my list of candidates for the 'coldest WR station' award. There was strong competition from Swindon, where like Brunel, 'I have long since ceased to take anything if I can avoid it', and Kemble, where the press-button electric fire would switch itself off just as you sat down after switching it on! Iver is a conglomeration of huts built of asbestos, corrugated iron and composition building blocks. The ticket office is at street level with only waiting rooms provided on the platforms which are in a shallow cutting. In later years it had an array of the black and white enamel signs and totems which were used on the WR for a short time when chocolate and cream went out of favour and before the new corporate image style was adopted.

Below: A perfect standard station of the 1898 type was Wargrave, as seen here with standard GWR seats, sheds, nameboard and fencing. *Author*

SOMERFORD

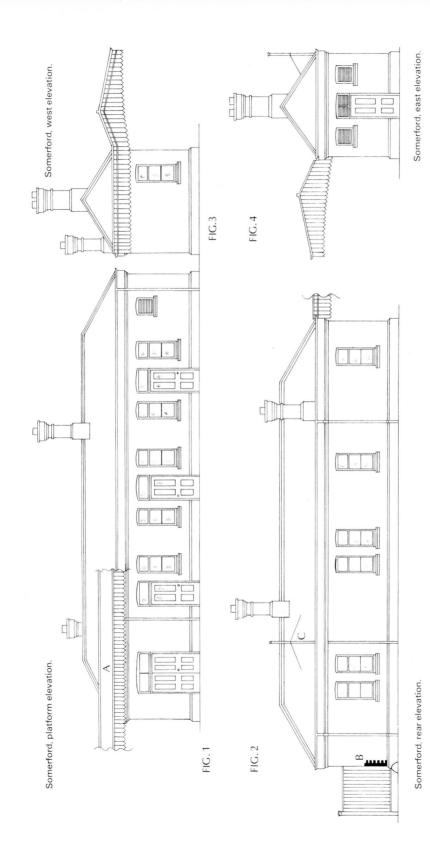

Somerford, west elevation.

Somerford, platform elevation.

FIG. 1

FIG. 2

Somerford, rear elevation.

FIG. 3

FIG. 4

Somerford, east elevation.

2mm : 1ft scale

Notes: (A) = Standard 'Invincible' glazing, (B) = Bullnosed engineers' blues, (C) = Metal vent pipe with metal stays.

51

Photo Survey : CHALFORD

Left: Eastbound freights passing Chalford made an impressive sight. Here, '28xx' 2-8-0 No 2817 attacks Sapperton bank in grand style. Note the stairs from the road overbridge.
Ian Allan Library

Below left: The Gloucester line sweeps down from Sapperton Tunnel in a series of curves and with a steep bank on the left. For this reason many signals in the Chalford area are on the 'wrong' side of the line to improve sighting. An auto-train waits in the loop by Chalford's standard signalbox on 14 September 1964.
B. J. Ashworth

Below: A down express hurries through Chalford while an auto-train waits to follow. The immaculate platforms are surfaced with 2in thick slabs and gravel, in standard fashion, but the doormats were not compulsory! *E. J. S. Gadsden*

Some Country Junctions

Many country junction stations on the Great Western developed into railheads for the surrounding district and grew to warrant a good service of main line stopping trains. As they developed, the station facilities were enlarged, often with quite disastrous consequences for the original structures which had assorted ill-matched extensions added. Chippenham, for instance, served the delightful Calne branch and possessed an attractive original building on the down platform. The up platform, an island, I remember as a shambles of canopies and unattractive buildings with the Calne branch bay awkwardly placed at the eastern end.

Kemble was certainly a local railhead and this has ensured its survival to the present day despite the loss of its branches to Tetbury and Cirencester in 1964. This was a particularly fine station dating from quite late in the 19th century and betraying some Elizabethan features although this style of structure had gone out of vogue by the time Kemble was built. Large buildings were provided on both platforms, with canopies carried on ironwork and glazed screens similar to the Ross-on-Wye type. It had some nice features which lifted it out of the ordinary though, notably the lattice footbridge with stairs integral with the buildings, and some large expanses of glazed screening. The latter were particularly attractive on the up platform where the buildings occupied the 'v' between the up main and the Cirencester branch, and the screens gave a cloister-like atmosphere around a triangular garden. In the late 1960s destruction of the Cirencester branch platform canopy ruined this feature, and the screens were reduced to low walls.

The Tetbury branch bay at the rear of the down platform was flanked by a long screen and canopy under which hung a sign 'Tetbury train' and an arrow to indicate where the train, latterly a diesel railbus, might be found. Further along the gravel surfaced platform a fox's brush hanging from one of the lamp posts reminded one that this was the heart of hunting country.

Kingham was similar to Kemble in that it formed a railhead, while only serving a very small village. It too, survives as a name on the rail map but all semblance to the fine station of the GWR era has gone. The lines to Cheltenham and Chipping Norton closed in 1962 and the mass of trackwork was gradually reduced to just the two through lines. The waiting shelter on platform four was similar to those at Shipton and Arley, the main buildings being an enlarged version of the Shipton type in cream bricks. Despite a considerable effort to save them, all were demolished in the mid-1970s and replaced by a utilitarian structure typical of the period.

Below: Yelverton, its timber buildings 'most queer and polygonal' (according to the poem) was a picturesque country junction. Now only rosebay and buddleia mark the site.

Another sad, but inevitable loss was the little station at Yelverton, where the branch to Princetown diverged. It is long gone now, with rosebay and buddleia covering the site. Here, the buildings were timber and reminiscent of Culkerton, but their island location in the fork of the diverging lines necessitated the curious five-sided plan. In a poem produced at the time of closure they were aptly described as 'most queer and polygonal'.

Some other West Country junctions were curious, too. At Liskeard, the Looe branch bay was virtually a separate station, with the branch running northwards and then turning through almost 360deg to reach Coombe Halt where trains were obliged to reverse in order to run south to Looe. The layout was made necesary by the location of Liskeard on a hill surrounded by deep valleys and the Looe branch still uses this unusual arrangement.

Further west, at St Erth the St Ives branch is provided with a bay platform slightly lower than the adjacent up main line platform. The effect adds to the interest of this neat station of Cornish stone which still retains much of its atmosphere. There are many more country junction stations deserving of a mention — Yatton with its fine B&ER signalbox, and Yarnton with its strange metal framed waiting shelter — for instance, but space precludes more than a glimpse of a few examples.

Above: The country junction *was* important as a traffic feeder. In this 1952 view of St Erth crowds have just piled off the branch train from St Ives to make connection with the up train arriving behind 'Britannia' Pacific No 70019. It is April and the holiday season is just beginning . . . *B. A. Butt*

Below: A quiet corner of St Erth station with the railcar for St Ives waiting at the lower level bay platform. *Author*

Above: Kemble station seen at its best in 1963, with a typical Gloucester-Swindon local train making connection with the Cirencester branch railbus. *R. N. Joanes*

Below: A standard goods shed and signalbox were features of Brent station, seen here on 31 August 1954 with a Kingsbridge branch train departing. Note the wording of the station nameboard. *J. F. Oxley*

Right: A wealth of detail is visible in this view of the signalbox, engine shed, and water tank, at Kingham. On the right is the branch to Chipping Norton and Banbury. *N. Caplan*

Below: The decline in the status of Kingham station is reflected in the replacement of these fine early standard buildings with basic modern facilities. *R. M. Casserley*

Bottom: The 16.05 Hereford-Paddington arrives at Kingham. The impressive lattice girder footbridge connected at its far end into the grounds of a hotel. The far waiting shelter is similar to those at Shipton and Arley. *B. J. Ashworth*

Photo Survey : DULVERTON

Below: Like Kingham and Kemble, Dulverton was an interchange station without any significant local centre of population. This 1963 view shows plenty of interesting detail. Modellers should note the curious shape of the office on the extreme right, complete with a safety barrier outside the door. *R. C. Riley*

Top right: The road approach to Dulverton, seen after closure. The nearer part of the structure was a substantial house with the station offices occupying the far single-storey section. *Author*

Centre right: A busy scene at Dulverton. The covered lattice-girder footbridge and standard timber signalbox are both text-book examples of their type.

Bottom right: An Exe Valley train leaving Dulverton. The main points of interest in this photograph are the 1950s era lamps (guy-wires and overhead power supply for cheapness sake), and the base of the signalbox which has been rebuilt in brick. *R. E. Toop*

Subsidiary Buildings

During the early part of the century standardisation also spread to many of the station components and fittings, much of the metal work being cast in the Swindon foundry. Thus while other systems used old rail for station nameboard posts, the GWR produced an elegant circular cast iron post which could double for other uses, and was frequently to be found supporting the wooden screens of gents' toilets. Some nameboards, too, were cast iron. Initially the board and lettering was cast as a unit, but later sans-serif letters were cast individually and screwed to a timber board. Seat ends, cast first with the monogram, and later with the GWR circlet, were also a product of this era. Prior to the cast nameboards, incidentally, the GWR had used blue and white enamelled plate nameboards, enamelling on metal sheet having come into vogue during the latter years of the Victorian era. These boards are now museum pieces but a fine example survives at Bewdley on the Severn Valley Railway.

The smallest and most well-known of the GWR standard buildings were the so-called 'pagoda' sheds. These were introduced around 1907 and gained their name from the curious shape of the roof. The first

Left: Black Dog Halt on the Chippenham-Calne branch was the private station of the Marquis of Landsdowne until the early 1950s, and although the public were allowed to use it, it was not included in public timetables. *P. Strong*

Below left: 'Carriage approach to the station. Foot passengers under the bridge' A relic of bygone years at Black Dog in 1964. *Author*

Top right: A yard office or store of fairly typical design. Slightly unusual in having a tiled roof. Staines West, 1980. *Author*

Centre right: An unmistakable product of GWR standardisation, the weigh office, complete with machinery and H. Pooley weighing platform, still surviving at Handborough in 1979. *Author*

Bottom right: Standard stable block at Chipping Norton, latterly converted to house a motor lorry. Brickwork in English bond with alternating courses in red and blue engineers' bricks. *Author*

examples appear to have been steel framed, with the wall cladding of concrete or steel sections and this type existed at Newbury West Fields as a halt shelter, and as a cycle shed at Kemble. The production version which is so familiar to GW followers was clad with corrugated iron, and painted in light and dark stone colours. The pagodas were supplied in kit form by Joseph Ash & Sons of Birmingham and carried the makers name on a blue and white enamel plate over the doors. The normal arrangement had a double door in the front, with a window each side, but some were without windows, some had three sets of doors and others had doors in both sides. They were used frequently as sheds, particularly for cycles, and also as waiting shelters for station platforms such as Adlestrop and Loudwater, and halts.

The construction of halts in quantity stemmed from the railmotor experiments between Gloucester and Chalford in the first years of the 20th century. The halt structure, consisting of a basic platform and shelter would be located near a group of houses or a country lane to provide 'bus-stop' facilities and to counter road competition. The platforms were constructed either from a series of timber frames surfaced with old

Left: Standard stable block at Shipton for Burford. This example, in red brick is unusual in having the floor well above mean ground level, probably due to problems of drainage from the field at rear. *Author*

Below left: A 'pagoda' shed in its most usual form. This was the cycle shed at Fairford. *M. S. Cross*

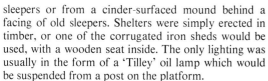

Right: Top to bottom: Ship-lapped timber waiting shelter, Kintbury. Typical brick waiting shelter, Shipton. Free-standing awning on cast iron columns, Bewdley. Timber goods office, Shipton. *All Author*

sleepers or from a cinder-surfaced mound behind a facing of old sleepers. Shelters were simply erected in timber, or one of the corrugated iron sheds would be used, with a wooden seat inside. The only lighting was usually in the form of a 'Tilley' oil lamp which would be suspended from a post on the platform.

Stanley Bridge Halt on the Calne branch was a typical cinder platform with a pagoda shelter. Appleford, which still survives, has this type of shelter on a framed platform, as did Horspath and, Rollright Halts, and Rodmarton platform on the Tetbury branch. The title 'platform' seems to have been used quite indiscriminately, and a halt might consist of a bare platform, while some 'platforms' such as Wootton Wawen had quite substantial buildings. Two nice examples of timber halts with timber shelters were Yeo Mill on the Taunton-Barnstaple line, and Combe Halt near Oxford.

Halt building continued up to the 1960s, though the number built after Nationalisation was quite small. Cassington Halt on the Fairford branch was opened in 1936 and was built entirely of concrete. This material did find favour on the GWR in the late 1930s for platforms and some structures, but never to the extent that the neighbouring Southern Railway used it for fencing and even nameboards. Concrete framing was used for new or lengthened platforms, and there were examples at Eynsham and Chalford. Two concrete halts were provided on the Staines branch with the opening of Poyle Estate Halt in 1954 and Colnbrook Estate Halt in 1961. Both served industrial estates, and the latter lasted only four years, before the line was closed. The Western Region also provided rail level timber platforms at several locations on the Tetbury and Cirencester branches in connection with railbus operations which began in 1959 and survived until 1964.

Inevitably, many of the country stations which were reprieved from closure have been reduced to unstaffed halt status, their buildings replaced by bus shelters and their once pristine platforms now overgrown.

Above: A standard timber-framed platform with one of the later-type corrugated iron shelters at Weston-under-Penyard Halt on the Wye Valley line. In BR days the shelter was unusually painted in a blue/green shade. *B. J. Ashworth*

Below: Halts offered only basic 'bus-stop' facilities. Post and wire fencing with white handrails was standard, as seen here at Cashes Green Halt. *B. J. Ashworth*

Above: Standard timber-frame platform, but with a simple wooden shelter. The down platform at Combe Halt, near Handborough. Note the Tilley lamp hanging from its wooden mast. *K. A. Jaggers*

Below: A murky morning in 1958 finds a diesel railcar on a rush hour working at Foley Park Halt, Kidderminster. The small wooden building appears to be a ticket kiosk, and the battens across the platform ramp are an anti-slip measure. *Anthony A. Vickers*

Photo Survey : STANLEY BRIDGE HALT

Above: Wiltshire Pastoral. A Derby 3-car unit glides past Stanley Bridge Halt. The massive nameboard is on timber posts — cast columns were not used at lowly halts. *P. Strong*

Below: Stanley Bridge Halt had a pagoda shelter on a timber-faced cinder platform. A wintry mist covers the countryside, and the nameboard has gone, indicating recent closure. *Author*

In sharp contrast is this view of Stanley Bridge Halt in 1964 with a Calne-bound train departing. The halt served only a few farms. *Andrew Muckley*

Above: Churchs Hill Halt was built to serve the village of Culkerton when diesel railbuses were introduced on the Kemble-Tetbury branch. The vehicles were fitted with retractable steps for easy access from the low platforms. *M. G. D. Farr*

Below: Few modern versions of the traditional halt were built, but curiously two were provided to serve industrial sites adjacent to the West Drayton-Staines West branch. Poyle Estate Halt, seen here on the day it closed, was similar to its sister at Colnbrook Estate. *Author*

Signalboxes

The earliest methods of train signalling with strategically placed railway 'policemen' and later with crude signalling apparatus meant that the signalbox was not ordinarily found among original GWR building designs. The first recognisable examples appeared during the latter half of the 19th century, and among the most common signalbox designs was the type erected by the signal engineering company, Saxby & Farmer. This style was distinctive in having oval 'toplight' windows above the main window frames, and was not peculiar to the GWR, being found on many systems where Saxby & Farmer installations were used.

A late survivor of this type, though not at a country station, was the Dainton Summit box, while the station box at Cheddar (shown in the B&ER section) is also of the same pattern. St Ives signalbox originally had the oval toplights but these were later panelled over and this may have been the fate of other S&F signalboxes. At Silverton the platform-mounted S&F box survived until late, despite being replaced by a more modern box. Many of the early signalboxes were overtaken by events, however, and alterations to track layouts, quadrupling, or signalling developments rendered them obsolete very quickly.

To replace them the Great Western produced a distinctive standard design which was constructed from the latter years of the 19th century until after

Above: A perfect example of a standard signalbox, this one was at Bedwyn, seen in 1978 shortly before it succumbed to a resignalling scheme. *Author*

Below: Tenbury Wells' curious signalbox and waiting room combination perhaps owes its odd appearance to its GWR and London & North Western Railway Joint ancestry. The main station building is shown in a later chapter. *R. J. Leigh*

Above: Aynho station box, seen here with 'Grange' 4-6-0 No 6871 passing on a southbound express, was a standard box built into the station platform.   *S. Creer*

Below: Oxford North Junction was one of several austere wartime signalboxes in the Oxford area.   *J. D. Edwards*

World War 1. The main identifying features were a hipped roof with metal vents, and windows having five panes of glass, three small above two larger ones. Stairs could be inside or outside, usually depending on the size or importance of the box, and the provision of inside or separate outside sanitary facilities was similarly dependent. The windows extended across the full front of the box and usually along both sides, and most of the frames had provision for sliding. These sliding casements fitted behind a top batten but there was often no bottom 'runner', just a row of dowel pegs driven into the sill. Where signalmen were required to lean out of windows, for example when exchanging tokens without the use of lineside apparatus, a 1in diameter metal rail was fitted across the outside of the window aperture.

There were too many of these boxes for it to be worthwhile singling out specific examples as being of particular merit, but the varieties of usage are worth a mention. The design varied in height to provide the best possible vantage point for the signalman, with structures such as the Yarnton Junction box being unusually high. Some examples such as Aynho station, were platform-mounted, as was Brimscombe before the surrounding platform was removed. Many examples were built of wood, some such as Colnbrook presumably in the interests of economy, but other timber examples were quite large and at important locations. More usually the structure was in red brick with bull-nosed engineers blues for all angles, matching exactly the standard station buildings of the period. At

Above: Savernake East signalbox was a small example of the simplified standard box. *Author*

Below: A nice platform-mounted example of the simplified type was the signalbox at Bromyard. A lovely atmospheric picture, in which you can almost feel the dampness. Note the 'over-growth' of lupins from the station garden! *W. G. Sumner*

Photo Survey : BRUERN CROSSING

Three views of the standard timber signalbox at Bruern Crossing
near Kingham. *Author/T. G. Flinders*

Taplow and Marlborough there were late examples built of pressed concrete or asbestos panels.

A simplified signalbox design was also widely used, possibly appearing somewhat later than the previous type. The signalboxes on the Oxford-Worcester line, some on the Berks & Hants, and at Calne, for instance, are of this type. Here, the brickwork was in brindled red and blue engineers bricks, with standard joinery although not usually having the five paned windows, and with a simple gable roof. Steps were usually outside, and led to an external landing with a porch. Good examples still survive at Ascott-under-Wychwood and Moreton-in-Marsh. There was a platform-mounted version at Bromyard, and a tall example still survives at Ledbury.

Signalling modifications carried out immediately before and during World War 2 usually incurred the construction of one of the austere 'modern' GWR boxes built of pink brick with metal window frames and a concrete slab roof. A number in the Oxford area were of this type, being built to control extended freight yards, while the doubling of track and lengthening of passing loops on sections of the ex-Didcot, Newbury & Southampton line saw most of the boxes on that route replaced by the new type. A derelict example still stands at Burghclere.

New signalboxes built during the 1960s by the Western Region employed pre-fabricated construction in natural timber finish, and were particularly handsome. There were examples at West Drayton and Shiplake, and the rebuilt Hungerford box was also of this type.

Above: One of the Western Region's stylish timber signalboxes, at Keynsham & Somerdale East. *Ivo Peters*

Below: Savernake West signalbox, minus chimney stack, in 1978. *Author*

Goods Sheds

The country goods shed is a structure which took on its distinctive, and readily recognised form right from the earliest days of the railway. The requirement for covered accommodation with an unloading platform and a simple means of transferring goods to a road vehicle was recognised from the outset, and since they were a prominent feature of the railway landscape, good architectural design was important. It would have been easy for the tiny Brunel 'roadside' stations to be overpowered by the visual intrusion of a badly designed goods shed nearby, and such incongruity was never part of his vision of the Great Western.

So, the goods sheds were designed either to match, or to complement the station architecture. There was ample opportunity, on a building with the fairly substantial proportions of a typical goods shed, to expand the Elizabethan Gothic style with pointed arches and window apertures. The end result had probably more resemblance to the village church than to its intended purpose.

A fine example of such a goods shed was the little red brick structure which matched the 'roadside' station at Culham. It stood in the yard at the Oxford end of the station, on the down side, and was solidly built with mock-Tudor brick and stonework and in perfect harmony with its surroundings. It has gone now and the present collection of modern structures

belonging to nearby laboratories are a perfect example of the visual intrusion of some modern architecture into the landscape. This is exactly the situation which, 150 years ago, the architect was at pains to avoid.

The photograph of Coates goods shed shows an example of this early type, constructed entirely of stone, and somewhat the worse for wear, having lost its roof. Coates was situated a little further down the Gloucester line from Kemble and although the latter was the passenger station, Coates served as a freight railhead for the surrounding villages.

These days it is not easy to find one of these 'ecclesiastical' goods sheds in anything like original condition, but the one at Stroud is an exception, although somewhat larger than usual. Fate and the elements seem to have been unusually kind to this old stone structure which still looks much as it must have done when new. Curiously, its most noted feature nowadays, is not the splendid architecture but rather the retention of one of the Great Western's immortal slogans emblazoned on the main wall. In fact, such a brazen disfigurement would never have been tolerated by Brunel and was most probably applied as a cheap form of advertisement during the years of depression in the present century.

Many of the other original goods sheds were built in timber, to complement rather than to match the station building. Over the years these have become known as the 'broad gauge' sheds although they were no more confined to the broad gauge than their stone or brick counterparts. The largest concentration of them seems to have occurred between Oxford and Worcester, but there were others in similar style, at Aldermaston, for instance.

The timber sheds were a far cry from the brick variety in that they lacked any embellishment, and their closest kin were probably the typical blackened timber barns of the period. A single railway track passed right through the building, via round-topped arches in the end walls, and served a central loading platform. On the opposite side of this platform similar archways were provided for road vehicles. The platforms were usually built of timber, but brick or stone were sometimes used.

During the 1950s some of the buildings were repaired and the shape of the archways over the rail entrance was altered. The drawing accompanying this chapter shows both the original and revised shapes. The timber walls were erected on concrete footings into which lengths of bullhead rail were cast to provide the supporting spurs. These footings and the sawn off rail sections were still visible in 1979 at the site of Chipping Campden and Shipton goods sheds. The best surviving example of this style is the broad gauge transfer shed preserved by the Great Western Society at Didcot. It differs in detail from the conventional

sheds, and had a standard gauge track in place of the road vehicle access.

Later GWR goods sheds were often built in brick, in a style which matched the 1898 station designs. Two good examples at Brent and Tetbury are illustrated and the latter still survives, as does the similar shed at Maidenhead. Combinations of red and blue bricks were used to good effect, and standard joinery was provided for the doors and windows. The latter had the shallow curved brick arch which was a feature of the matching station buildings. Lighting had evidently been a problem in some of the earlier sheds, and this was overcome by providing a glazed gable end and often a substantial glazed skylight in the roof. The office still took the form of a lean-to at one end although additional office accommodation was often provided internally with a timber-built structure on the platform. Although the rail track still passed right through the building, the road vehicle facilities now consisted of a loading bay with an opening in one side wall protected only by an external awning.

The goods shed at Culkerton, on the Tetbury branch, featured the standard brickwork and joinery but had an external siding and platform which received minimal weather protection from a high awning. The exposed position of this building, on an embankment in open countryside must have made it a very draughty place to work. The road vehicle loading bay was reached through a doorway in the main structure which gave access to a cut-away area in the internal platform. The accompanying illustrations show the structure as it was after the track had been lifted and new doors had been fitted on the road entrance.

Few country goods sheds survived long after closure, as there were few uses which could be found for them. Colwall, Bourne End and Kidlington now form light industrial premises, Much Wenlock is a coal store, and Bewdley and Bridgnorth provide covered accommodation for restoration of preserved rolling stock.

Above left: Noteworthy early GWR goods shed at Stroud. Note the stonework, arches, and wall buttresses, and the rebuilt chimney stack. *G. Scott-Lowe*

Below: Coates Goods, near Kemble, stands gaunt and derelict with the loss of its roof adding to the impression of a ruined priory church. The detailing of the roof and window of the lean-to office are quite perfect. *M. G. D. Farr*

Above: A goods shed built of ragged stone, this is Much Wenlock in 1979. *Adrian Knowles*

Above left: Culkerton goods shed employed items of standard joinery in an unusual little building which was full of character. *Author*

Left: The road vehicle entrance and lean-to office of Hungerford's broad gauge era goods shed. *Author*

Below: A diesel railcar hustles into Wells City station past a most attractive goods shed of local Mendip stone. *E. W. Field*

Above: The transfer shed at Didcot had a standard gauge siding in place of the road vehicle access. Although it is an important relic, it differed from most of its contemporaries in having vertical boarding. Additional roof bracing has been added. *Great Western Society*

Left: An example of a 20th century goods shed designed for a location where little traffic was anticipated. This is the goods 'lock-up' at Little Somerford, typical of those on the South Wales direct line. *K. R. Willows*

Below left: The standard pattern goods shed design from the last years of the Victorian era. This example at Tetbury still exists. *R. J. Leigh*

Above: Main wall detail of the timber goods shed at Shipton for Burford. The concrete footings are visible, but on this example there are no external supporting spurs. *P. H. Wells*

Below: The slate battens and some internal framing are visible in this 1964 view of the 'broad gauge' goods shed at Evesham being dismantled. *Anthony A. Vickers*

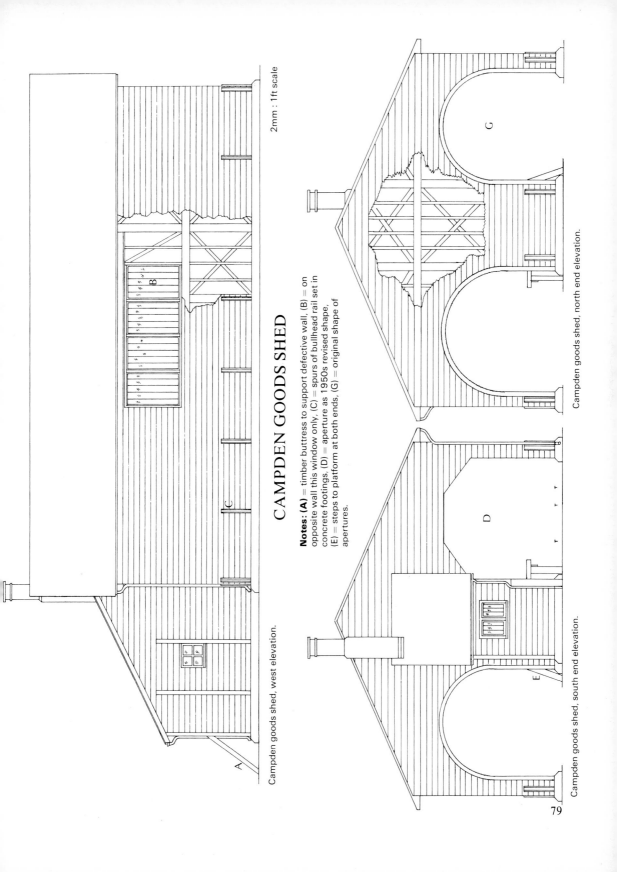

CAMPDEN GOODS SHED

2mm : 1ft scale

Notes: (A) = timber buttress to support defective wall, **(B)** = on opposite wall this window only, **(C)** = spurs of bullhead rail set in concrete footings, **(D)** = aperture as 1950s revised shape, **(E)** = steps to platform at both ends, **(G)** = original shape of apertures.

Campden goods shed, west elevation.

Campden goods shed, north end elevation.

Campden goods shed, south end elevation.

Inherited Station Buildings

Above: A cobbled approach road and a lovely decorated frontage distinguished Kidderminster station. Perhaps if it had been a public house and not a station it would still be with us. *Author*

Although the widespread use of standardised architecture gave the Great Western's territory its own characteristic personality, there were many inherited designs which added their own special contribution. Some came from small independent beginnings and were swallowed by the GWR even before their first train ran. Others were the product of larger schemes, some of which were promoted by the GWR from the outset while others made a meagre living in spite of the Great Western and were then thrust into their larger competitor's camp at the Grouping.

One of the three north-south routes across GWR territory was that of the Didcot, Newbury & Southampton Railway which also had distinctive architecture. The DNS employed two-storey cottage style buildings and the stations and crossing keepers' dwellings were in the same style. The houses had barge-boards cut with an intricate pattern, but the most distinctive feature was the use of a small gable over each of the upstairs windows giving a semi-dormer effect. Several still survive in private use, and a good example is Compton Crossing, where the house retains a number of railway features.

The rambling 25-mile long Fairford branch was the product of two railway companies and the buildings on the section from Yarnton to Witney (old) were built of timber. The intention of the East Gloucestershire Railway was to build westwards from Witney to Cirencester but the impetus petered out in a field near Fairford which remained the line's terminus until closure in 1962. With the exception of Kelmscott & Langford all the EGR stations were built to a similar design, including the new station at Witney, which was the only example to be provided with a canopy, albeit an entirely free-standing timber one.

The Alvescot building was constructed in red brick but all the others, including Witney, were in Cotswold stone. The long, narrow bungalow structures with their thick walls and small windows were quite unlike any others on the Great Western. Fairford possessed a stone-built goods shed, a turntable and engine shed, and after closure in 1962 it remained derelict for some years before the site was cleared and an agricultural depot built there. The station itself has been converted to form offices. At Witney the old station was used as a goods office and since the Oxford-Witney goods service remained in operation long after passenger services ended, the old timber station outlasted its new neighbour by several years.

Many country station buildings were combined with a substantial house providing accommodation for the stationmaster. These tended to occur in quite large concentrations in some areas, such as the West Midlands, and on some of the Welsh lines, notably the Cambrian. Furthermore, during the 1920s and 1930s the GW launched a drive to create more staff accommodation and as a result surplus space in a number of stations was converted into private dwellings. With the wholesale closures of the Beeching era, many of these rural properties became surplus and because they often provided substantial accommodation many were snapped up at bargain prices and now form fine private dwellings.

Dulverton is one example, although because of its isolated position it stood abandoned and derelict for several years before being sold. Now the main building and the goods shed remain and the track bed and site of the down platform form a lawn. The station house here was large and the elevations were unusually hung with grey slates giving a rather drab appearance.

More delightful, and still to be enjoyed in their original guise, are the stations of the Severn Valley Railway. This part of the West Midlands abounds with the station/house type buildings and many are still in existence. On the preserved section of the SVR, Arley and Hampton Loade are similar in style and built of yellow brick under a slate roof. Bewdley and Highley are expanded versions of the same type, the former in red brick and the latter in local stone. Highley is a

Above: This outside-framed timber station building at Shipston-on-Stour was probably original, although the platform facing appears to have been rebuilt to GWR standard. *Author*

Below: The rugged stone cottage-style buildings of the East Gloucestershire Railway, were quite unlike anything else on the Great Western. Fairford, seen here on 2 March 1968, has since been converted to form offices. *Author*

particular favourite of mine, and I am doubly fortunate in having known it before preservation. Today it retains all its old charm, with hanging baskets and lots of GW trappings to enhance the scene. Only the lattice GW footbridge which provided a quick exit to the village is missing, although gas lamps and GW paintwork have been restored.

A similar single-platform example to Highley was at Much Wenlock, and here the yellow brick station house was also built in 'Severn Valley' style. The branch from Wellington crossed the Severn Valley line at Buildwas Junction, which in its heyday must have been a fascinating place. There is little local habitation, and the station took its name from the nearby ruined abbey, but it provided an interchange point for lines in four directions.

It used to be possible to walk up from Buildwas through Farley Dingle on the 1 in 40 gradient of the old track bed to Much Wenlock. The station here was in a sylvan setting, enhanced by the fact that the goods yard was further on and hidden from view beyond a curve in the track.

Perhaps we should not move on from this area without mention of some other buildings, some of which still survive. The tiny bungalow buildings at Rushbury and Harton Road were both converted, but while Rushbury was linked to its signalbox with new construction to form an attractive dwelling, Harton Road was taken over by a local farm and became a stable! Cressage has formed an impressive country house, and at the time of my last visit Berrington, Coalport, Neen Sollars, Cleobury Mortimer and Wyre Forest were all in use as private houses.

The Wycombe Railway favoured the station/house style for its buildings on the Maidenhead-High Wycombe line which is now sadly severed at Bourne End. Here, and at Cookham, the original buildings have been rather mutilated in the interests of modernisation, although to be fair Bourne End was not in original condition, having been substantially extended when the branch to Marlow was built. Wooburn Green and Loudwater were more attractive, the former now being a private house, while the latter

Left: The pink sandstone buildings of the Taunton-Minehead line were unique to that line, and happily they still survive. Stogumber's curious ground-level building is now part of the West Somerset Railway, but the goods shed and timber platform have gone. *Michael Hale*

Below left: A 1958 view of the East Gloucestershire Railway Cotswold stone station at Lechlade. It was still in original condition with square chimney pots and a roof-less gents toilet. *E. Wilmshurst*

Below: A Devonshire station and goods shed in local stone. This is Bovey Tracey in May, 1939. Note drain pipes on platform as flower tubs. *Richard Gee*

has been demolished. The construction, though unusual in railway buildings, is a familiar feature of churches and cottages in this part of the Home Counties, being formed of red brick plinths and corners with walls of knapped flint construction.

The Taunton-Minehead branch matched its neighbour from Taunton-Barnstaple for both scenic appeal and delightful stations. Thanks to the West Somerset Railway some of the once derelict stations on the Minehead branch are now restored and these include the picturesque stone structure at Dunster. However, the tiny pink-sandstone bungalows should not be passed by, and that at Stogumber was high on my list of favourites. Here, the stone offices are at ground level and on the opposite side of the line from the platform. This was a ramshackle timber affair surmounted by a timber waiting shelter. It has been largely demolished by the WSR as it was beyond repair but it will be a great pity if the replacement structure cannot preserve a little of that delightfully 'backwoods' character.

Many and varied are the uses to which redundant stations have been put, and the lovely Cambrian building at Three Cocks Junction now forms the offices of the area depot for Calor gas. This delightful old building was a cement-rendered cottage, latterly painted chocolate and cream but betraying evidence of an earlier repaint in the experimental green colour

Left: A grand red sandstone house with a little station attached is Highley, now preserved by the Severn Valley Railway. *Author*

Below left: Railcar No W22W in BR green livery loads parcels at Cleobury Mortimer in 1961. The station is typical of those in the Severn valley area. *E. T. Gill*

Above: The bold and imposing frontage of Tenbury Wells looks not quite Great Western and betrays a hint of the LNWR influence. *R. J. Leigh*

Below: A general view of Tenbury Wells in 1962, by which time it was rather larger than its traffic demanded. *W. G. Sumner*

Photo Survey : ST IVES

Above: St Ives was predominantly a passenger station, with a long platform but only two short goods sidings. There is still a railway-owned hotel in this popular resort. *C. J. Blay*

Below: The small goods shed at St Ives, tucked in under the cliffs. *Author*

Above: St Ives from the air, with the engine shed and viaduct, bottom left.

Below: This rear view of the station shows the rugged construction in Cornish granite. There were similarities with the station at Helston. *S. W. Stevens-Stratten*

scheme which was used in this area. A feature of this building was the licensed refreshment room, complete with wooden pump handles on the bar. The upper floor provided private accommodation. Thirsty travellers in this area will be pleased to find that the former Talyllyn Junction station is now the 'Talyllyn Arms' while to the north, Builth Road Low Level became the 'Cambrian Arms' after closure.

The black and white half-timbered frontage of Kidderminster had tremendous appeal, and I well remember arriving there at dusk on one occasion when it presented more of the appearance of a village 'pub' than a station. Parts of the structure had developed a 'list' which made it appear far older than it really was, and indeed there is some interesting speculation about its origins. The first Kidderminster station was devastated by fire and it is thought that the 'new' building was destined for a more auspicious site such as Stratford-upon-Avon, when the fire occurred and the design and prefabricated parts were diverted to Kidderminster as an emergency measure. Its destruction occurred with indecent haste on the discovery of dry rot in the timbers, and the red brick and glass box which replaced it is certainly in keeping with local architecture but can hardly compensate for the loss of a fine building.

Photo Survey : DN&SR

Left: The Didcot, Newbury & Southampton Railway was less fortunate than the MSWJR and was operated from the outset by the Great Western, as witness the nameboard, signals and token catcher in this early view of Upton & Blewbury. *LPC/Ian Allan Ltd*

Below left: Now a private house, Upton & Blewbury still possesses all its DN&S features. *Author*

Right: Elaborate barge boards and tiny gables identify this as a DN&S structure even without its ground frame nameplate and lamp. *Author*

Below: Still the same style, but with different barge boards, this is Highclere on the day before passenger services were withdrawn. *Derek Cross*

Left: A lovely piece of typical Buckinghamshire knapped flint walling was the Wycombe Railway's standard design as seen here at Loudwater. *Author*

Below: A slightly retouched composite photograph showing Loudwater station from the station yard. *Author*

Bottom: The closure of the Bourne End-High Wycombe section in 1970 ended the Wycombe Railway's usefulness as a cross-country and diversionary route, and caused much controversy. Five years afterwards only a litter-strewn trackbed and a derelict shell of a building remain at Loudwater. *Kevin Lane*

Photo Survey : MUCH WENLOCK

Much Wenlock station seen in the early years of the present century, still sporting a variety of original features. Although the twisted chimney pots and painted nameboards were later replaced with more orthodox GWR fittings, the curious water column remained until the station closed.
Shropshire County Museums

This was a particularly fine station building, well suited to its location in the ancient Borough of Wenlock close by the ruined abbey. Much Wenlock remains a most attractive town, marred only by some peripheral housing development, and yet throughout its life the railway which served it seems to have been a forgotten GWR backwater. The section between Craven Arms and Much Wenlock closed to passengers in 1951. Hardly surprising since it served only the tiny villages of Presthope, Longville, Rushbury, and Harton Road. From then until it, too, was closed 10 years later, Much Wenlock became passenger terminus of the branch from Wellington, with an occasional freight trip as far as Longville.

I first visited Much Wenlock in 1964, shortly after the line had been lifted, and the station building was empty and derelict. It was a grand structure in pale cream bricks and similar in design to some of the preserved stations on the Severn Valley Railway. The major part of the building was a dwelling house having three downstairs rooms, a kitchen and entrance hall. Upstairs there were three bedrooms, and a bathroom with dressing room adjoining. A single storey section

at the Buildwas end contained various outbuildings and had been extended to provide a coal shed. The latter had not been keyed in to the original brickwork adequately and was falling away badly. It has been removed during renovation of the building.

All quoins and window apertures were of dressed stone, and the grey slate roof was capped with cast iron ridge tiles carrying a fleur de lys motif. Massive terra-cotta chimney pots with a spiral pattern were originally fitted but these were later replaced by smaller square ones. The single-storey section contained all the 'railway' offices, porters' room, ladies waiting room, booking office and an open-topped gents' lavatory. On the platform side, a small canopy was carried on cast iron brackets.

Close examination of the structure revealed that a similar canopy on the roadside had been removed at some stage. The road elevation also shows evidence of the removal of a door and installation of a window of slightly different dimensions. The platform surface was in diamond-treaded engineers' blues except for the area beneath the canopy which was a chequer pattern of red and black tiles. Both were standard methods of

91

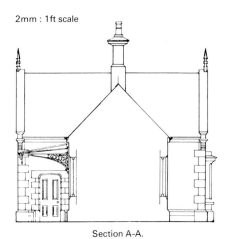

Section A-A.

paving in the Victorian era and my previous home in Windsor (built 1883) had paths in both styles.

Internally, the building was not very remarkable, but the wooden screen wall with Gothic arches, in the booking office was a pleasant touch. Early photographs of the structure, now in the Much Wenlock Museum, show a pointed obelisk over the booking office. This could have been a clock or bell tower but all trace of it had disappeared, apparently by the time of World War 1. One of these photographs is a very early view of the station, with four-wheel coaches in the platform, but unfortunately it was not suitable for reproduction.

The accompanying drawings depict the station as it was during its last years and have been reproduced from site measurements and photographs. For the

sake of clarity the ridge tiles are omitted from the main drawings.

In 1978 work commenced on the renovation and conversion of the station to provide private dwellings. The station house remains largely in original condition, with missing sections of ridge tiling replaced and renewed doors and windows in keeping with the original. The office section has been imaginatively converted to form two split level dwellings, with alterations to some doors and windows in matching style, and the addition of a number of skylights in the roof. A recent view of the structure is included in the concluding section of this book.

The Much Wenlock branch was usually worked by a '41xx' class 2-6-2T or a '57xx' class 0-6-0PT in later years, but had earlier been a stronghold of the '44xx' class 2-6-2Ts whose small wheels gave them an advantage on the 1 in 40 climb through Farley Dingle. For many years a couple of these locomotives were housed in the attractive engine shed at Much Wenlock. It is perhaps a little curious that none of the buildings here were in matching style, although since the station stood in splendid isolation from the yard it was unaffected. The engine shed, built of multi-coloured bricks, was long enough to house the 70ft railmotor which once worked the line, and had a large water tank mounted on the roof.

The goods shed, illustrated on page 76 was a small and rather crude structure in grey stone with a corrugated iron extension at one end. A standard pattern red brick signalbox was provided by the GWR to replace the original. This appears to have been the small timber building at the Presthope end of the platform, which remained in use as a staff mess room.

2mm : 1ft scale

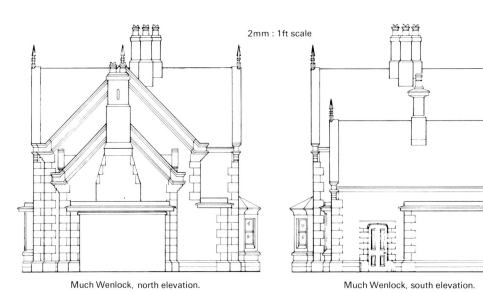

Much Wenlock, north elevation.   Much Wenlock, south elevation.

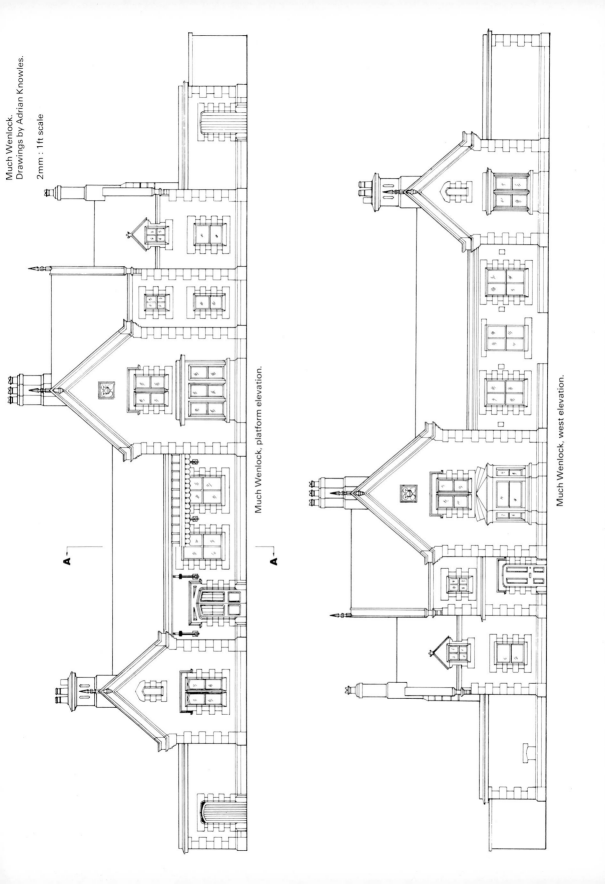

Much Wenlock.
Drawings by Adrian Knowles.

2mm : 1ft scale

Much Wenlock, platform elevation.

Much Wenlock, west elevation.

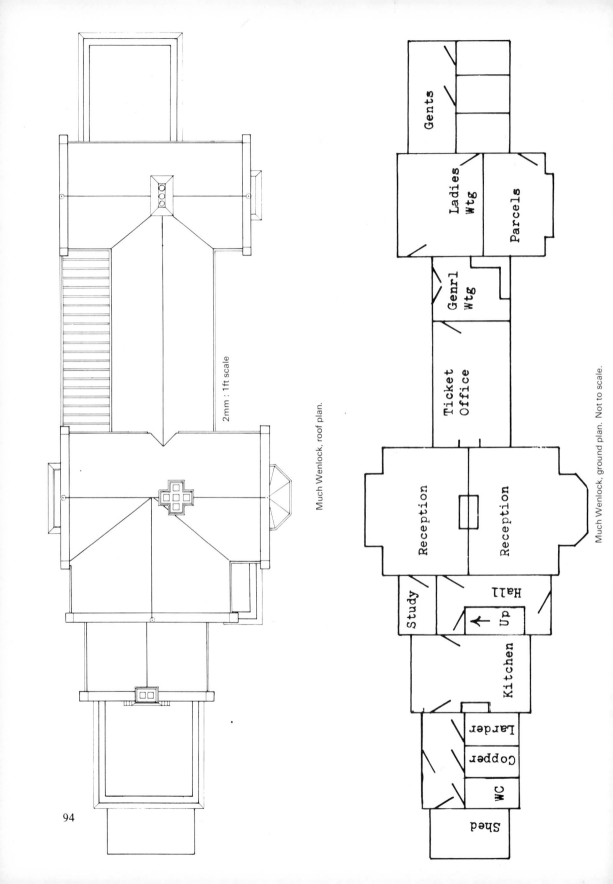

2mm : 1ft scale

Much Wenlock, roof plan.

Much Wenlock, ground plan. Not to scale.

94

Above: Looking towards Buildwas in 1959, with all the trappings of Great Westernry, although the concrete nameboard posts were unusual.   *F. Hornby*

Below: It was this splendidly atmospheric photograph, taken on 1 April, 1962, which first prompted me to visit Much Wenlock.
M. A. Schumann

Top: Details of Much Wenlock canopy brackets, ridge tiles and chimney stack (left). The 'Gothic' screen (right) in the booking office.

Above: View from the road approach showing the extensive stonework, and the bricking in Flemish bond. The station remained in GWR colours and was not repainted until restoration in 1978. *Adrian Knowles*

Midland & South Western Junction Railway

Above: Cirencester Watermoor in MSWJR days, with lamps and nameboards very different from the GWR types.
LPC/Ian Allan Library

The Marquis of Ailesbury was a major landowner in the Savernake Forest area, and the second station at Savernake, later known as High Level, was built at his insistence when he permitted the Midland & South Western Junction Railway to bypass the B&H station by building a new line across his land. The new station was to be 'adjacent and at least equal in accommodation to the existing GWR (B&H) station'. MSWJR stations, with the exception of Cirencester and Swindon Town, were rather mean little bungalow structures and the Savernake station proved to be no exception although it did have a private waiting room for the Marquis. Although they were simple, reflecting the MSW's lack of funds, many of its structures were very attractive, and the buildings at Savernake and nearby Grafton still survive as private dwellings. The former has had so many extensions that little of the original is now recognisable, but the Marquis' waiting room serves as a garden shed and there are two other interesting structures in the grounds. The wooden signalbox is used as a summerhouse and drawings of this are included later in this chapter. It is almost certainly the only MSWJR signalbox in existence and its all-wood construction would make it an ideal project for removal to a preservation site. Nearby stands the original water tank and this too is an attractive building. The tank, manufactured by Stothert & Pitt of Bath and still bearing its GWR 'stone' paintwork is mounted atop a brick-built engine-house which once contained the small pump engine

which filled the tank. Examination of this building in the late 1960s gave me my best 'close encounter' with a rather surprised barn owl!

Elsewhere, little remains of the MSW station sites. My favourite was Cricklade, which still had its track in place when I first visited it. The station building was rather basic — a gable-roofed red brick structure with a simple canopy — but there was a large goods shed and a very nice little signalbox. The site is now a housing estate. Here, mention must be made of Swindon Town, that thorn in the very heart of the Great Western. It had three platform faces, and a large red brick station building. Part of this had two storeys and it also possessed a licensed refreshment room. Right up to the time of its slow and piecemeal demolition during the 1960s this place was worth a visit. There were two signalboxes, the south box being a typical MSW wooden structure, and the north a London & South Western type brick cabin built into the rock face close to the tunnel under the 'old' town. Swindon town station also had a goods shed, a turntable, and some interesting grounded coach bodies.

Photo Survey :
SAVERNAKE HIGH LEVEL

Left: The remains of the Marquis' private waiting room at Savernake High Level, much altered to serve as a garden shed. *Author*

Below left: The MSWJR water tank and pump house at Savernake. *Author*

Right: Savernake High Level signalbox, as featured in the accompanying drawings. This delightful timber structure still exists. *R. J. Leigh*

Below: Savernake's MSWJR station was a plain little structure, rather overpowered by an ugly canopy on cast iron columns. *R. C. Riley*

4mm : 1ft scale

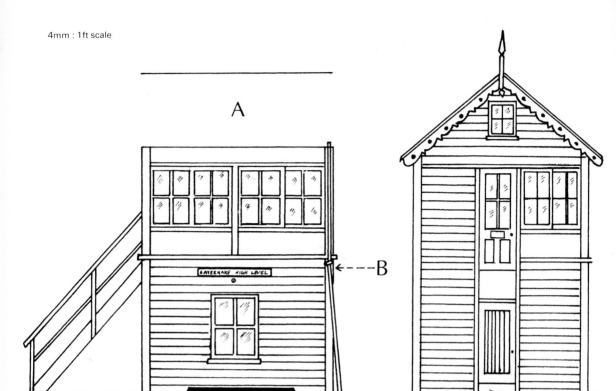

A

SAVERNAKE HIGH LEVEL

←---B

BEAM

Above: Savernake High Level signalbox, front and west elevations.

Notes: (A) = roof omitted to show top panel detail, (B) = operating floor level.

Below: Foss Cross, here seen on 5 July 1958, was probably the most remote, and least patronised of MSWJR stations. *E. Wilmshurst*

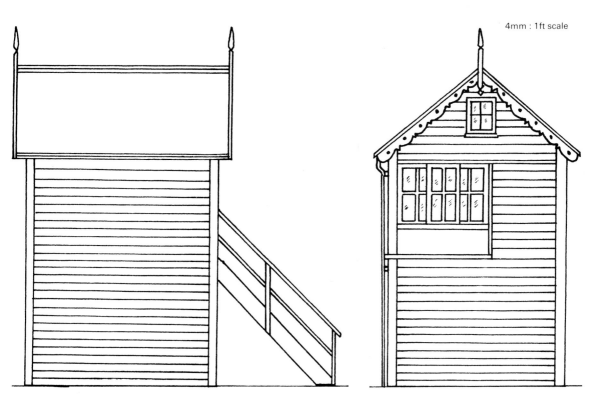

4mm : 1ft scale

Above: Savernake High Level signalbox, rear and east elevations.

Below: A most unusual sight at Foss Cross in June 1961 was this Swindon Cross-Country unit, apparently on a driver-training run. The track appears little-used, and the MSW line closed a few months later without ever being dieselised. *J. H. Dagley-Morris*

Bristol & Exeter Railway

Two distinctive and very different styles of architecture used by the Bristol & Exeter Railway are featured here. There may well have been others, but the B&E has never featured strongly in this respect in published histories, and the examples depicted here exhibit a number of very typical B&E features.

The drawings show the main station building at Bampton, built by the Tiverton & North Devon Railway and opened in 1884. The styling is pure B&E, with the same distinctive 'H' shaped plan as the stations at Cadeleigh, Wiveliscombe, Milverton and Up Exe, and possibly all these and other similar buildings may have their origins with the same local builder. There were subtle variations to the design, for instance, Milverton lacked the glass 'conservatory' at the front, and instead had an open-fronted waiting shelter. The highly decorative timber barge boards were probably the most distinctive feature, although in the case of Bampton, these were replaced by the Great Western with plain boards. The drawing shows one gable fitted with each type.

The two early photographs of Bampton reproduced here are worthy of close study. Note the extent of the horticulture — even a lean-to greenhouse was provided. The waiting shelter, with its 'Gothic'

windows survived until the station was closed, and was rather smaller than usual.

The Cheddar Valley line pre-dates the Exe Valley by some 20 years and it too, had its own style of architecture. The line was the result of an agreement between the B&ER and the Somerset & Dorset Joint Railway. The former wished to build a line from Bleadon to Wells, while the latter was seeking a way into Bristol. The two agreed that the B&E should build a line from Wells to Yatton and in due course the Cheddar Valley & Yatton Railway Act was passed on 14 July 1864. A subsequent Act of 19 June 1865 authorised the B&E to build and operate the single broad gauge line. It was opened between Yatton and Cheddar on 3 August 1869 and through to Wells in April of the following year.

The buildings were of local Mendip stone and the rugged construction was relieved by typical B&E decorations. There were the usual decorative barge boards, station names carved in stone, and a roof in red tiles with alternating bands of plain and patterned tiles. These were generally six courses of 'saw-tooth' pattern tiles and four courses of plain. The ridge tiles carried a cruciform motif, but these were much smaller than the fleur de lys pattern used by the builders of

Above left: The lovely B&ER station at Cadeleigh, with matching station house immediately beside it. The double-sided nameboard seems rather odd. *R. C. Riley*

Top: Axbridge has a timber waiting shelter typical of the Cheddar Valley line, with the name prominently displayed. *R. E. Toop*

Above: Congresbury station is typical of the B&ER architecture on this line. It was built of Mendip stone and with much decorated roofing. *R. E. Toop*

Above: A dmu from Barnstaple arrives at Milverton, a station which has now disappeared under road improvements. The waiting shelter is similar to that at Axbridge. *H. A. Dunn*

Below: Cheddar had a particularly fine stone station building with a train-shed betraying Brunelian influence. In this 1963 view the roof span has been propped with stout timbers. *D. H. Ballantyne*

Much Wenlock station, and were made of tile clay rather than cast iron.

The building at Cheddar was much larger than those provided at the other stations, as considerable tourist traffic was anticipated. In fact, apart from tourists and strawberries, Cheddar generated very little traffic but in late Victorian days the area was a favourite holiday haunt. Unfortunately, it was popularised by the 'better-off' and in the early years of this century these folk found the area within easy reach of their new-found mobility in the form of the motor car. The charabanc operators too found it a ready market, while access by rail involved changing trains at Yatton or Witham. The train service was leisurely, and of the intermediate stations only Wells had any real traffic potential.

The line closed to passengers in 1963 but remained in use for occasional freight traffic some while after this. Cheddar station retained its train-shed until closure, but had lost it by the time of my visit in 1965/6 although a single line of track remained in situ.

Above: The Saxby & Farmer signalbox and rugged stone goods shed at Cheddar. *R. E. Toop*

Below: A view from the station yard after the train shed had been removed. The twisted terra-cotta chimney pots were a feature of B&ER buildings. *Author*

Photo Survey : BAMPTON

Above: A splendid early view of Bampton, with an 0-6-0ST heading 4- and 6-wheel coaches on a northbound train. The details are worthy of close study, but note particularly that the station garden incorporates dwarf hedges, a pond, and even a statuette! *Rev D. M. Claridge*

Below: Another early view of Bampton, this time looking south from the road bridge. This is a more recent view, the most obvious changes being the growth of trees, a new platform surface and two new chimney pots.
Bucknell Collection/Ian Allan Library

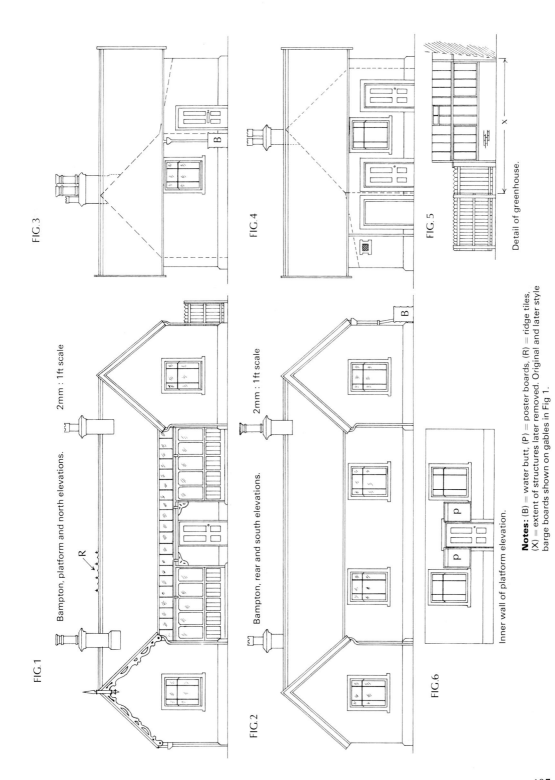

FIG.1

Bampton, platform and north elevations.

2mm : 1ft scale

R

FIG.2

Bampton, rear and south elevations.

2mm : 1ft scale

B

FIG.3

FIG.4

FIG.5

Detail of greenhouse.

X

FIG.6

Inner wall of platform elevation.

P   P   P

Notes: (B) = water butt, (P) = poster boards, (R) = ridge tiles.
(X) = extent of structures later removed. Original and later style
barge boards shown on gables in Fig 1.

107

Berks & Hants Extension Railway

The Berks & Hants line, between Reading and Westbury, began life with the blessing of the GWR, initially as a single line of broad gauge to Newbury. The Berks & Hants Extension Railway, which despite its name was almost entirely in Wiltshire, then built onwards through Hungerford and Pewsey. Eventually, of course, this became the main line to the West of England and its piecemeal development over many years resulted in a splendid variety of architecture. Yet, while its motive power was recorded in infinite detail, and every schoolboy learnt the story of its crack express, the 'Cornish Riviera', its architectural niceties were largely obliterated during the 1960s, unwritten but well remembered.

The Brunel chalets at Theale and Aldermaston have already been mentioned, and further west the line developed a style more its own, with neat buildings at Midgham and Hungerford. Kintbury was timber-built and rather ramshackle, but from Bedwyn on to Woodborough the buildings were a soft pink colour in Elizabethan style. These were not, however, related to the Brunel 'roadside' stations although aspects of the styling were similar. The B&HER structures varied in size to suit their location, with Woodborough and Bedwyn being the smallest and consisting of little more than a small booking office and waiting room. Bedwyn had a tiny canopy, which was really no more than a porch over the booking office door. Savernake was the best looking example, with a recess on the platform side supported by timber columns and beams. Pewsey was a larger version of Savernake and its slightly squat appearance was not enhanced by rather short chimney stacks. It is now the only survivor of the type. Further details of the Savernake building are given in the notes accompanying the drawings.

At Savernake and Hungerford the station facilities were enlarged by the provision of a second platform on which there was a standard GWR building of the 1898 type. At Hungerford this was on the up platform, and the realignment of tracks here left the original down platform building in a curious position standing at a skew angle to the platform edge. Savernake had its new building on the down platform.

Below: In this 1960s view of the diminutive Berks & Hants Extension Railway station at Woodborough, the facilities have been expanded with timber and brick outbuildings. The goods shed dates from the broad gauge era. *P. Strong*

Right: An early view of Woodborough in which some 20 members of railway staff have turned out for the photographer. *P. Strong Collection*

Below right: Pewsey station was one of the larger examples of B&HER architecture. *Author*

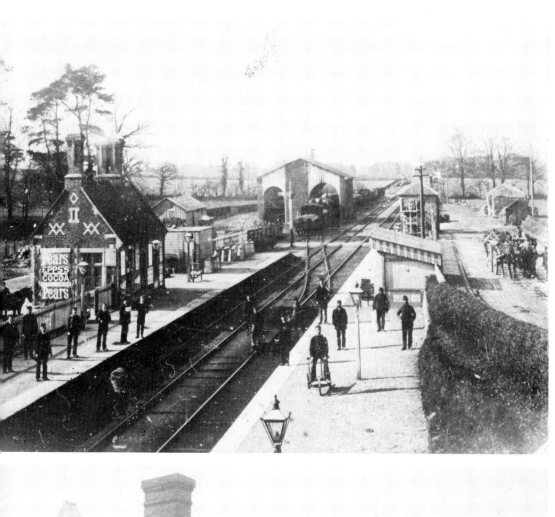

Above: A two-car dmu for Westbury pauses at Savernake Low Level in the summer of 1964. The decorative patterns in the brickwork were similar to those on the nearby hotel. *R. J. Leigh*

Right: Roof details of Savernake Low Level, seen from the road bridge in 1964. *Author*

The station building, on the up platform, was built of pinkish red bricks with a decoration of cream bricks to match the adjacent Savernake Forest Hotel. The recessed area on the platform side was carried on wooden beams with a plain timber post. The roof was of grey slate and all the gables were capped with stonework. The gents toilet was originally open-topped, and the adjacent exit passageway later became a parcels and cloakroom. Note that three classes of waiting room were originally provided. The gothic arches to the main door were an attractive feature. A tilley lamp bracket and winding mechanism was provided on the platform side of the building, but electric lamp standards of 1930s era concrete pattern were provided on both platforms. These carried the rectangular GWR 'tablet' signs. An original drawing of this structure shows the estimated building cost as £1,118, certainly not cheap for a building of its day.

2mm : 1ft scale

Above: Savernake Low Level, north elevation.

Below: A farewell view of Savernake taken shortly before demolition, with the MSWJR signalbox just visible to the right of the nearer chimney. The hipped roof over the toilet is not original. *Author*

Above: The end elevation showing clearly the patterned brickwork in Flemish bond. Note the Tilley-lamp post and the unusual storage place for the ladder.   *R. J. Leigh*

Above right: Savernake Low Level, west elevation.

Below: Savernake Low Level, platform elevation.

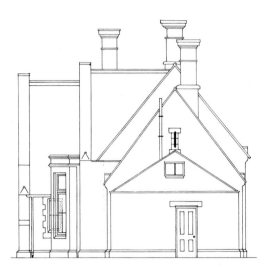

Notes: (CT) = cast trespass notice, (H) = hearth, (P) = poster board, (S) = season tickets must be shewn notice. Gents shown in final condition, originally had open top. Exit was converted to parcels & cloakroom.

2mm : 1ft scale

PLATFORM ELEVATION

A   Detail in Recess   B

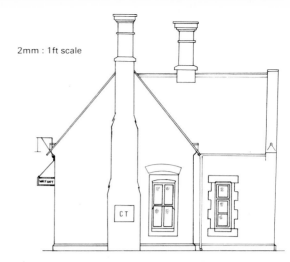

2mm : 1ft scale

Right: Savernake Low Level, east elevation.

Below: The down platform building at Savernake was this standard GWR hipped-roof structure, the nearer end of which was linked to the footbridge roof. *Author*

Bottom: Savernake Low Level, ground plan.

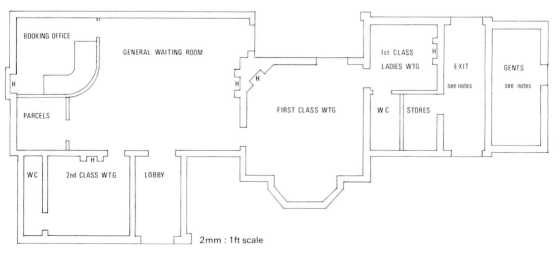

2mm : 1ft scale

113

Oxford, Worcester & Wolverhampton Railway

The Oxford, Worcester & Wolverhampton Railway had a short and troubled history as an independent company before being absorbed into the GWR system. The Great Western had backed it from the outset but in the early days of its construction it was crippled by a general economic depression. Construction costs then exceeded the estimates, and when the GWR refused to guarantee any more than £1,000,000 in additional construction costs, the OW&W Directors considered that they had been let down.

As engineer to the OW&W Brunel had frequently been in the middle of disputes between the two companies and the contractors who had been brought in to build the new line. Following the so-called 'Battle of Mickleton', in which Brunel led an army of navvies to seize the Campden tunnel works from the contractor, and amid mounting criticism of him by the OW&W board, Brunel resigned and John Fowler took over to complete the construction.

The architecture of the line, particularly in its timber goods sheds and 'chalet' style station buildings, was distinctly Brunelian. However, the extensive use of timber is unusual in view of his penchant for using local materials wherever possible, and the abundance

of available 'Cotswold' stone. In all probability the parlous financial state of the OW&W accounts for the almost exclusive use of timber in the construction of its buildings. The very 'basic' nature of the smaller buildings, which initially lacked even basic sanitary facilities for men, is probably also a result of lack of funds. The design of these small structures is also less typical of Brunel and they may well have been adapted by Fowler from a basic Brunel plan-form.

A number of these basic OW&W stations survived into the mid-1960s, including those at Handborough, Ascott, Chipping Campden and Fladbury. The joinery and main dimensions were standardised, but there were variations in the placing of doors and in the size and position of the flat-roofed extension. Further buildings of this type were constructed by the OW&W but traffic outgrew them during the latter part of the 19th century and they were replaced by standard GWR buildings. The survivors appear to have undergone a few modifications, and these were mainly undertaken in their later years. All were provided with a gents' toilet in a separate structure. A typical example was at Adlestrop, where a small brick structure was constructed on the up platform. The style of brickwork suggests that this dated from the period when OW&W buildings were being replaced by GWR structures. An early drawing of the basic OW&W buildings shows only the central chimney, and the floor plan shows a store room occupying one corner. Most of the structures acquired a second chimney, placed in this corner, which suggests that the internal arrangement was modified at the same time. The door to the store room from outside was also either sealed or removed. The exterior view of Chipping Campden shows this doorway blocked by the battery cupboard.

Ascott-under-Wychwood station building was extended in matching style to provide additional accommodation. This station and Adlestrop and Campden, were repainted in BR standard chocolate and cream following removal of the canopies during

Left: '28xx' class 2-8-0 No 2820 has steam to spare as it wheels a train of empty coal wagons through Handborough in June 1955. *J. Woolfenden*

Top right: The typical OW&W timber station building at Fladbury. *Lens of Sutton*

Centre right: Great Western crossing gates in original form with metal bars instead of wire mesh, at Ascott-under-Wychwood in about 1912. *Packer's Studio*

Below: Handborough in the early 1960s complete with all its buildings and some unusual Tilley-lamp posts. *Lens of Sutton*

115

Top: Moreton-in-Marsh in the 1930s after closure of the Shipston branch. The black goods shed and island platform waiting room are original, but the main station building is an early GWR standard type. *Lens of Sutton*

Above: Littleton & Badsey was something of a curiosity, its outside-framed timber building resembling the GWR standard type, and very similar to Culkerton on the Tetbury branch. *H. I. Quayle*

Right: The waiting shelter at Moreton-in-Marsh was shorn of its canopies during the late 1950s, like all the OW&W timber buildings. *Dr A. L. Ross*

Top: The OW&W timber station at Ascott-under-Wychwood was extended by the Great Western to provide dwelling accommodation. The door and windows of the extension did not match. *K. A. Jaggers*

Above: ' . . . and on the platform only the name . . . ' The 11.32 to Oxford finds no passengers at Adlestrop on 18 May 1963. The goods shed is disused. The platform shows both original and later surfaces. *Michael Hale*

the 1950s, but Handborough remained in GWR light and dark stone until demolished. At the time of the funeral of Sir Winston Churchill in 1965 it was in a poor state and had weathered to a yellow/brown colour. When used as a terminus for the funeral train, it was draped in purple and white cloth over the roof and walls.

All these stations were scheduled for closure in the Beeching Report, but Handborough and Ascott escaped by being reduced to unstaffed halts. Both buildings were demolished soon afterwards. The stationmasters' houses at Handborough and Adlestrop and the signalbox at Ascott, all built by the GWR, still stand but there is little else at any of these sites.

118

Photo Survey :
CHIPPING CAMPDEN

Left: Chipping Campden still sporting its original, rather ungainly, chimney. *Author*

Below left: The original OW&W waiting shelter and timber goods shed. *Lens of Sutton*

Top right: An early view of Chipping Campden, apparently taken from the signalbox. *Lens of Sutton*

Centre right: Original GWR gates and lamps at Chipping Campden level crossing in 1954 as 'Castle' No 5090 *Neath Abbey* passes with an up express. *D. E. H. Box*

Below: The road side of the down platform building in about 1964. The battery cupboard fills an original doorway and it seems likely that the extended awning also once protected a doorway. *R. J. Leigh*

ADLESTROP

In the summer of 1898 an express train made an unscheduled stop at this quiet wayside station on the border of Oxfordshire and Gloucester. The poet, Edward Thomas happened to be a passenger on the train, and the deserted station with its curious name prompted him to write a short poem. He captured the spirit of the place and the feeling of that brief stop so well that the little station was assured a place in history.

I went there only once. The weather was grim and the main purpose of the visit was to walk to Stow-on-the-Wold station. I joined the ticket queue at Oxford among a large group of people who were booking to Paddington. When my turn came I requested a return to Adlestrop, only to receive, like everyone else, a return to Paddington! When I rejected this, there was

a short flurry of activity before the booking clerk produced the correct item. To my delight and amazement it was boldly marked '3rd class', some 10 years after the abolition of third class seating.

I travelled by diesel unit to Combe halt, where despite it being nearly mid-day, the Tilley lamp was still in position hanging from a high post on the platform. Storm clouds were gathering and, agitated by a rising wind, the burning lamp made a loud hissing

Above: Adlestrop, looking east, showing the various sheds and the brick gents on the up platform, and on the extreme right the GWR pagoda shelter. *G. Biddle*

Below: The Edward Thomas poem as displayed in Adlestrop bus shelter. *R. I. Wallace*

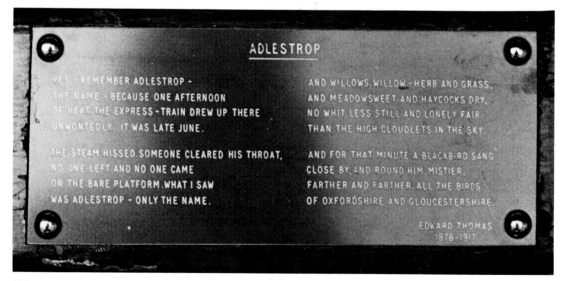

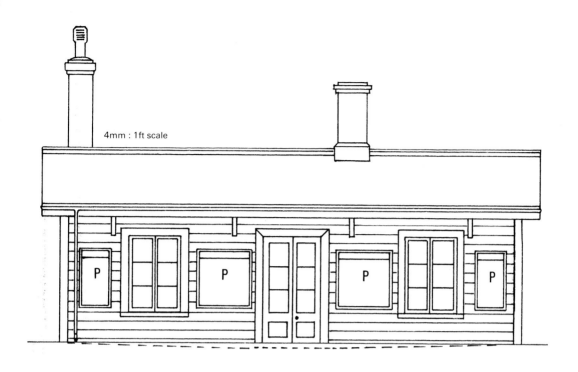

4mm : 1ft scale

Adlestrop, platform and rear elevations.

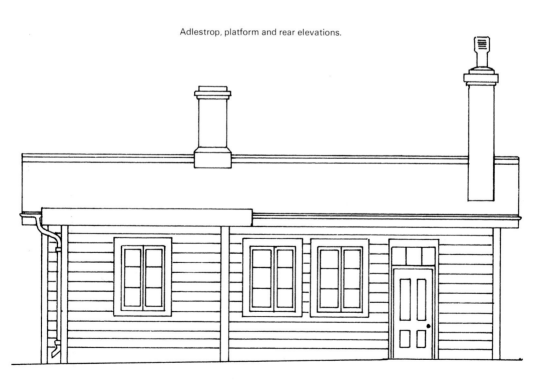

121

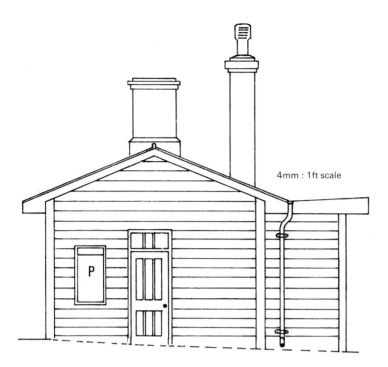

4mm : 1ft scale

Left: Adlestrop, east elevation.

Below left: Adlestrop, west elevation.

Below: End detail of canopy.

Right: Adlestrop, ground plan.

Below right: Station staff parade for the photographer as a down express passes on an unknown date in the early 1930s. *Packer's Studio*

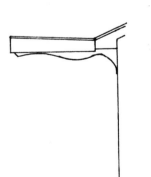

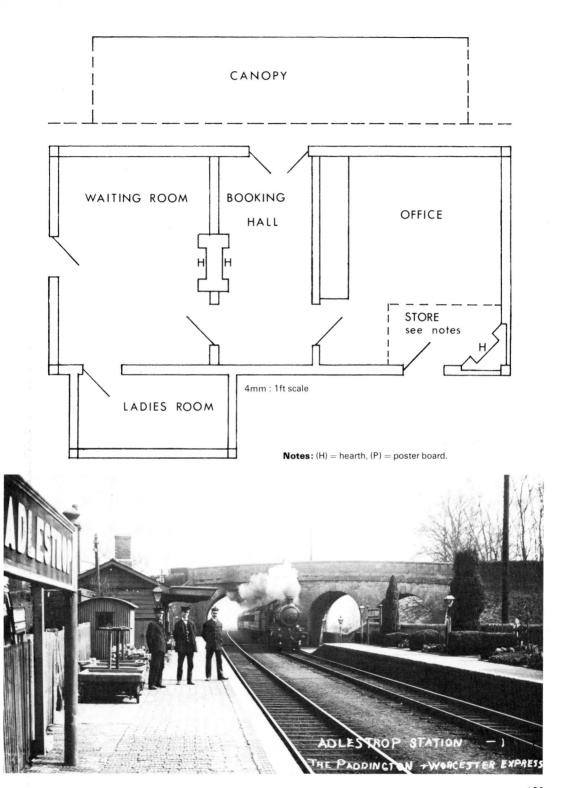

CANOPY

WAITING ROOM

BOOKING
HALL

OFFICE

H H

STORE
see notes

H

LADIES ROOM

4mm : 1ft scale

Notes: (H) = hearth, (P) = poster board.

ADLESTROP STATION   — 1
THE PADDINGTON → WORCESTER EXPRESS

Above: The station house at Adlestrop with the river Evenlode in the foreground, and the railway, now single-track, behind it. *Author*

noise. We 'flagged' the usual 13.25 Oxford-Moreton and on this occasion the two Hawksworth coaches were headed by BR Standard Class 5MT 4-6-0 No 73162, in less than perfect condition. The rather jerky ride through the Evenlode valley ended when we alighted at Adlestrop under a black sky and in pouring rain.

The location is surrounded by woodland and the down platform, a mixture of diamond-treaded engineers' blues and gravel, possessed one of the ubiquitous 'pagodas' as its only shelter. This was one of the classic shelters, devoid of windows and leaning a shade drunkenly towards the track. Like the rest of the station it was painted in WR cream.

The main OW&W building was on the up platform, neatly kept but by then stripped of its little wooden canopy. Alongside and to the rear were corrugated iron store sheds of the larger curved roof type, very common on this stretch of line. The improvements dating from the early GWR era were fairly obvious, being betrayed by the brickwork and standard joinery. The original low OW&W platform had been raised to near normal height, but dropped away to the booking office door, as shown on the drawing. A gents' urinal was provided in a separate brick-built structure at the Worcester end of the building, and the main chimney stack had been rebuilt and a second stack added. On

the down side of the line to the rear of the waiting shelter a railway house was provided. This delightful cottage was distinguished by alternating courses of red and grey bricks, GWR windows, and an array of 'railway' chimney pots.

At the time of my visit, only the concrete footings remained of the timber goods shed, which had stood at the Worcester end of the up platform. Adlestrop was closed to passengers on 3 January, 1966, and was demolished soon afterwards. A station seat and nameboard were removed to the village and placed on display. Subsequently they were housed in a bus shelter, together with a small plaque carrying the words of Edward Thomas's poem. Nothing now remains of the station buildings although the site is easily distinguished by the presence of a few sections of wooden paling fence. Happily, the cottage still survives, tucked away down a leafy gravel track and reached by a small wooden bridge over the infant River Evenlode.

124

A Special Favourite

Of all these fine old buildings, it is inevitable that there should be one which occupies a special place in one's affections. In my case, and perhaps it is only right, that special station was less than a mile from my childhood home and was the starting point for many of the excursions which provided the substance for this book. What a place! A rambling Georgian 'barn' built more than 10 years before the GWR, of which it eventually became part. Staines West was a comfortable home for a Quaker family who owned a mustard mill in Staines at the time when Queen Victoria came to the throne. It was enlarged in the 1850s with a new wing and servants quarters, and in 1880 was acquired by the Staines & West Drayton Railway as the site for their terminus.

The little S&WDR ran out of money when its line was half finished. It bought the rails for the Colnbrook-Staines section on the principle of 'live now — pay later', and eventually decided that a new station building at Staines was beyond its means. The big house on the site was converted with the addition

Above: The Georgian mansion which formed the station at Staines West was one of the most curious buildings inherited by the Great Western. The small windows under the eaves are in attic rooms once occupied by the servants. *Author*

of a new booking hall with double doors, and a platform and canopy where the garden had been. Internal alterations were initially of a minor nature, although subsequent modifications to provide two upstairs apartments have made it impossible to be certain of its original form. Two marvellous features remained throughout until the time of writing this, though. The staircase rose from the booking hall and had a gate marked 'Private' at its foot, and the 'kitchen' door was sealed shut and fitted with a ticket window!

After passenger services were withdrawn in 1965,

the upper parts of the station remained occupied as private flats. By the mid-1970s there was only one tenant still in residence and the building was increasingly subject to vandalism. The author became involved in efforts to secure the future of the building at this time, and the long struggle is not ended yet. This is not the place to retell all of that, but suffice to say that station conservation is not for the faint-hearted.

You needed to know this building in order to love it, and to most people it must seem a rather gaunt and unattractive pile. It occupies an imposing street-corner position on the edge of the town's Conservation Area, which was re-drawn to include the station and its platform and canopy. All around it, a once seedy and run down area has been restored with some buildings well treated and others ruined. The station is now the only major eyesore. Yet, but for the interest of a few stalwarts, it would almost certainly have been demolished in 1977 when dry-rot infestation was discovered.

It was hastily declared uninhabitable, the sole remaining tenant moved out, and the structure was left to the vandals. At this time it was already a Listed Building, described by the Department of Environment as 'an interesting amalgam of domestic and railway architecture'. Eventually it was sold to the local authority for the token sum of £1, but the transaction took two more years which the station could ill afford, and even then there was no sign of anyone who actually *wanted* to lease and restore the structure under the authority's terms. That is, as commercial offices.

By Christmas 1979 the station had become an object lesson for anyone who thought that dry-rot eradication is a problem which can be left waiting. Many of the windows were open to incursion by vandals and the floor, long unsafe, had collapsed leaving gaping holes through to the cellar. The final chapters in the history of Staines West will doubtless be written during the 1980s, and we can but hope that the place will survive in some form.

Above: Staines West seen in 1960, when still in GWR 'stone' paintwork. This was originally the front of the house and the area now covered by track and platforms was a large garden. Shortly after this picture was taken the station was repainted in an unusual combination of WR cream with forget-me-not blue.
F. J. Saunders

COUNTRY STATION
CONVERSIONS

Above: Blagdon, on the Wrington Vale Light Railway, April 1978. *G. F. Roose*

Below: Rushbury, station and signalbox, 1979. *Adrian Knowles*

Bottom: Much Wenlock after renovation, 1979. *Adrian Knowles*

Index

Page numbers in italic type refer to photographs

Adlestrop 115, *117, 120-124*
Aldermaston *21*
Alvescot 80
Ardley 48
Arley 81
Ascott-under-Wychwood 10, 73, 114, *115, 117*
Ashburton 15
Axbridge *103*
Aynho *30,* 70

Badminton *43-45,* 46
Bampton (Devon) 102, *106-107*
Bedwyn *69*
Bewdley *63*
Black Dog *60*
Blackthorn 48
Blagdon *127*
Blockley 50
Bloxham *2*
Bourne End 83
Bourton-on-the-Water 49
Bovey Tracey *83*
Box 30
Bradford-on-Avon *16*
Bramley 43
Brent *56*
Bridgend 15
Brimscombe *17*
Bromyard *71*
Bruern Crossing *72*
Buildwas 83
Builth Road 88
Burghclere 73

Cadeleigh *102*
Calne 73
Cashes Green Halt *64*
Cassington Halt 63
Castle Cary *46*
Chalford 11, 13, 49, *52-53*
Chard 15, *28*
Charlbury 15, 20, *26-27*
Cheddar 69, 102, *104-105*
Chepstow 15
Chipping Campden *79,* 114, *118-119*
Chipping Norton *61*
Chipping Sodbury 48
Churchs Hill Halt *68*
Christian Malford Halt 48
Cirencester Town 17, *19*
Cirencester Watermoor *97*
Cleobury Mortimer *84*
Clynderwen 30
Coates *75*
Colnbrook *7,* 11
Combe Halt *65*
Compton Crossing 80, *89*
Congresbury *103*
Cricklade *97*
Culham 15, 74

Culkerton 75, *76*

Didcot 75, *77*
Dulverton *58-59,* 81

Evesham *78*

Fairford 10, *62,* 80, *81*
Fladbury 114, *115*
Finstock 10
Foley Park Halt *65*
Foss Cross *100-101*
Frome 15, *29*

Grafton & Burbage 97
Grange Court 30

Haddenham 48
Hampton Loade 81
Handborough 10, *61, 114-115*
Hanwell & Elthorne 34
Harton Road 83
Hatch 15
Henley in Arden 13
Heyford 30, *31-34*
Highclere *89*
Highley 81, *84*
Hungerford 73, *76,* 108

Iver *49*

Kelmscott & Langford 80
Kemble 54, *56*
Keynsham & Somerdale 73
Kidderminster *80,* 88
Kidlington 30, *35*
Kingham 13, 34, 54, *57*
Kintbury *63,* 108

Lambourn 10, 46, *47*
Lechlade *83*
Ledbury 73, 75
Leigh Court 12
Liskeard 55
Littlemore *46*
Little Somerford 46, 51, 77
Littleton & Badsey *116*
Llangollen 43
Looe 10
Loudwater 83, *90*
Lustleigh *9*

Maidenhead 75
Malvern Wells *45*
Marlborough 73
Marlow 34
Melksham 15, *18*
Menheniot 15
Midgham 108
Milverton 102, *104*
Minety & Ashton Keynes *14,* 15

Moretonhampstead 15
Moreton-in-Marsh *13,* 73, *116*
Mortimer 15, 20, *22-26*
Much Wenlock 13, *76, 91-96, 127*

Newbury West Fields Halt 61

Oxford North Junction *70*

Pershore 34
Pewsey 108, *109*
Poyle Halt *4*
Poyle Estate Halt *68*

Rodmarton platform 63
Ross-on-Wye 34, *42*
Rushbury 11, 83, *127*

St Erth 55, *55*
St Ives 10, 69, *86-87*
Savernake 43, *71, 73,* 97, *98-101, 110-113*
Shiplake 73
Shipston-on-Stour *81*
Shipton for Burford 10, 34, *37-41, 62, 63,* 78
Shrivenham 15
Silverton 69
Staines West 11, 61, *125-126*
Stanley Bridge Halt 63, *66-67*
Starcross 17, *19*
Stogumber *82,* 85
Stonehouse 17, *18*
Stourbridge Town *10,* 34, *38*
Stow-on-the-Wold 49
Stroud 15, *74*
Swindon Town 97

Talyllyn Junction 88
Taplow 34, 73
Tavistock South *28*
Tenbury Wells *69, 85*
Tetbury *44,* 75, *77*
Theale *21*
Three Cocks *12,* 85

Up Exe 102
Upton & Blewbury 88
Uxbridge High Street *48*

Wargrave 43, *50*
Welford Park 46
Wells 43, *76*
West Drayton 73
Weston-under-Penyard Halt *64*
Witney 80
Wooburn Green 83
Woodborough *108*
Wootton Bassett *47*

Yelverton *54*
Yeo Mill Halt 63